The Acropolis
monuments and museum

By G. Papathanassopoulos
Ephor of Antiquities

KRENE EDITIONS

The statue of the cover page represents Athena from the pediment of the Giganto-machy:

The goddess, of a magnificent and unsurpassed aesthetic beauty, a masterpiece of the late archaic sculptured art (525 B.C.), stands with her left arm extended, and covered by the "aegis" and intends to kill her unrelenting opponent, Engelados, with the spear, which she is holding up in her right hand.

© *1977 by «KRENE» editions, Athens, Greece*

16, Vassilis St., Theseion - Athens, Tel. 34.75.012

All rights reserved, including the right to translate or to reproduce this book or parts thereof in any form

Translation: Helen Bacoyianis - Petronotis

**Printed and bound in Greece
by Ekdotike Hellados S.A.
8 Philadelphias Street — Athens**

PREFACE

One must begin with a hesitant hand, before undertaking the task of writing about the rock of the Acropolis, and especially, when this attempt is not a study, or a piece of research, but an effort to guide others in acquainting themselves with the most magnificent monument of all centuries, to bring them in contact with the high ideals that dominated the creators who expressed themselves through their works upon this rock.

In order to familiarize the visitor directly it seemed appropriate to use a Historical Diagram of the monuments, with the main dates and events that pertain to the historical process and fate of the rock through the centuries — from its earliest past, the Prehistoric period — to the present. Events and milestones in the history of the monuments which are directly associated with the political and religious lIfe of the people of ancient Athens, and of later dates, medieval, and more recent times, and which marked the fate of these monuments were noted in this diagram.

This guide-book basically, follows the order of presentation of the monuments of the sacred rock, as these were seen — in the middle of the second century A.D. — and described by Pausanias, the ancient traveller, in his "Attica".

Therefore, since reference is made to the rock and its fortifications, we follow the ancient roads, which encircle the Acropolis, and reach the monuments and shrines of the southern slope. Further on, following the same route, we stand before the shrines of the western and northern slope. Upon returning, we arrive at the gate and the monuments of the entrance to the sacred rock. A description of the main large monuments on the rock follows, as the visitor reaches each one during his walk, and the guide-book ends with the visit to the Museum of the Acropolis, which houses the priceless treasures of the sculptured decoration of temples, and shrines that have survived through the ages and are still to be found in Greece.

An insert has been added at the end of the text, in order to facilitate the traveller-tourist in following the proposed itinerary which, it was felt, is the most appropriate, and most inclusive in viewing the Acropolis, and its numerous monuments and shrines. The numbers in the text refer to the corresponding numbers on the insert.

With the permission of Mrs. Miliades, the statue of Athena, from the pediment of the Gigantomachy, was used on the cover, as it had been studied and reconstructed by John Miliades; a significant offer in the study of the sculptured embellishment of the monuments of the Acropolis.

HISTORICAL DIAGRAM

NEOLITHIC PERIOD 4000 - 3000 B.C. approximately

A settlement on the rock of the Acropolis, and on its northwest, west and southwest slopes.

EARLY HELLADIC PERIOD 3000 - 2000/1900 B.C.

The Acropolis continues to be settled.

MIDDLE HELLADIC PERIOD 2000/1900 - 1600 B.C.

The settlement expands to the slopes and around the rock. Middle Helladic graves to the west of the Erechtheion.

LATE HELLADIC PERIOD (Mycenaean)

16th - 14th c. B.C. The settlement becomes more densely populated. The "megaron" of the leader on the Acropolis.
13th c. B.C. Fortification of the Acropolis (Cyclopean wall). Additional fortified enclosure to the west and northwest of the hill (Pelargic wall).

SUB-MYCENAEAN/GEOMETRIC PERIOD

11th - 9th c. B.C. Expansion of the "Pelargic wall" to the west of the Acropolis.
8th c. B.C. "Enneapylon". The geometric temple of Athena on the site of the mycenaean megaron.

ARCHAIC PERIOD

682 B.C. Abolition of the institution of royalty in Athens. The Acropolis is no longer the center of royal authority.
636 B.C. Temporary occupation of the Acropolis by Kylon and his followers. "Kylonean taint".
6th c. B.C. (Beginning) Parthenon I (Hekatompedon).
570 B.C. Building of the "archaios neos" on the site of the old geometric temple of Athena.
566 B.C. Inauguration of the great Panathenaia. Building of the monumental ascent to the Acropolis.
540 B.C. The old temple of Dionysos is built on the southern slope of the Acropolis. Modelling of the level area in front of the temple, to meet the needs of the "dithyrambic choral cult dance".
6th c. B.C. (Middle) Installation of Peisistratos on the Acropolis.
510 B.C. The Peisistratid Hippias is expelled and obliged to forsake his home on the Acropolis. The Athenians teardown the greatest part of the Cyclopean wall in order to prevent a future installation of tyrants on the Acropolis.

LATE ARCHAIC PERIOD

490 B.C. Battle of Marathon. Commencement of the building of Parthenon II on the site of Parthenon I.
480 B.C. Conflagration and destruction of the Acropolis by the Persians. Victory of the Athenians at Salamis.
479 B.C. Themistocles build the fortification wall of the northern side of the Acropolis. Greek victories, against the Persians, at Plataiai and Mykale.
478 - 477 B.C. Creation of the first Athenian Confederation.
468 - 450 B.C. Probable continuation of the building of the Parthenon II by Kimon.
467 B.C. Kimon builds the fortification wall of the southern side of the Acropolis (Kimonian wall).
465 B.C. Following their victories against the Persians, the Athenians dedicate the colossal statue of "Athena Promachos" on the Acropolis.

CLASSICAL PERIOD

450 - 449 B.C. Kimon's death. With the prompting of Pericles, the Athenians decide to rebuild the glorious burnt shrines of the Acropolis.
447 B.C. Pericles begins the construction of Parthenon III.
445 B.C. Pericles builds the Odeum on the southern slope of the Acropolis.
438 B.C. Completion of the construction of the Parthenon. Official dedication of the temple, which coincides with the Panathenaic Festival.
437 - 432 B.C. The Propylaea of Mnesicles are constructed.

437 B.C. The beginning of the pedimental sculptured work on the Parthenon.

432 B.C. Termination of the work on the sculptural decoration of the Parthenon.

431 B.C. The Peloponnesian War begins.

429 B.C. Death of Pericles.

427 - 426 B.C. Temple of Athena Nike.

421 - 406/405 B.C. Erechtheion.

404 B.C. End of the Peloponnesian War.

334 B.C. Alexander the Great dedicates the persian shields, spoils of his victory at the Granicos river, to the eastern architrave of the Parthenon.

319 B.C. Choragic monuments of Thrasyllos and Nikias.

HELLENISTIC PERIOD

304 B.C. The Parthenon is used as the dwelling of Demetrios Poliorketes.

178 B.C. A pedestal with bronze quadriga is built by Eumenes the Second of Pergamum at the site of the entrance to the Propylaea.

2nd c. B.C. (First half) Eumenes the Second builds the Stoa, which bears his name to the west of the theater of Dionysos.

86 B.C. Pillage of Athens by the Roman general Sulla. Massacre of the defenders of the city, which had seeked refuge in the Acropolis. Aristion manages to burn the Odeum of Pericles before the Romans capture it and use its timber.

61 B.C. Ariobarzanes the Second of Cappadokia rebuilds the Odeum of Pericles, which Aristion had burnt.

27 - 12 B.C. The quadriga of Eumenes the Second is substituted by the quadriga of Agrippas, on the same pedestal.

17 - 10 B.C. The temple of Rome and Augustus on the Acropolis.

52 A.D. A monumental marble staircase is built on the site of the classical ascent of the Propylaea.

150 A.D. (or just before) Pausanias visits and describes the Acropolis.

160/161 A.D. Herodes Atticos builds the Odeum, on the southwestern slope of the Acropolis, in memory of his wife Regilla.

267 A.D. Invasion of the Heroulians. One of the central colonnades of the Parthenon is destroyed. Later on the Athenians fortified the western side of the Acropolis (Beulé gate) with a wall and towers.

LATE ANTIQUITY

361 - 363 A.D. Julian the Apostate restores the destroyed interior colonnade of the Parthenon.

5th c. A.D. Removal of the chryselephantine statue of Athena from the Acropolis, probably for the purpose of transporting it to Constantinople.

6th c. A.D. Transportation of the statue of Athena Promachos to Constantinople, during Emperor Justinian's reign.

CHRISTIAN PERIOD

The Acropolis is gradually transformed to a christian shrine:

— A large basilica is consecrated on the southern slope of the Acropolis, at the site of the Asklepieion.

— The Parthenon is transformed to the church of St. Sophia, and, later on, it becomes the church of "Panagia (Mary) Atheniotissa".

— The Erechtheion is transformed to a christian basilica, dedicated to the Mother of God.

— The Propylaea were transformed to a church dedicated to the Trinity (southern wing), to a church dedicated to the Archangels St. Michael and St. Gabriel (central axis), and were used as the see of the bishop of Athens.

— The church of the Holy Apostles was constructed on the site of the Clepsydra.

1203 A.D. Destruction of the statue of Athena Promachos in Constantinople, just before the latter was occupied by the Franks.

1205 A.D. Occupation of Athens by the Franks. The Acropolis is abandoned by the Metropolitan Michael Akominatos, who surrendered it to the Franks.

FRANKISH AND LATIN DOMINATION

1205 - 1456 A.D. The Acropolis is used once again as a fort by the Frankish and Latin conquerors, and is re-enforced with two observing-towers, one at the southern wing of the Propylaea (Koulas), and the other at the north end of the Acropolis (Belvedere).
— The Propylaea (Pinacotheca) were transformed to a two-storey palace, the headquarters of the Frankish prince, with an internal chapel of St. Bartholomew, while, even later, they became the "grand palace", headquarters of the Latin prince.
— The Erechtheion was also transformed later on to a palace of the Latin princes.
— The Parthenon become a latin church, dedicated to "Santa Maria di Athene", and, later on, by the dukes De la Roche, to Notre Dame.

TURKISH OCCUPATION

1456 A.D. Occupation of the Acropolis by the Turks. Through the years the entire form of the sacred rock alters. The areas between the monuments fill with houses, the Acropolis becomes a small settlement, and has a limited significance as a fort.
— The Parthenon is transformed to a mosque and, later on, to a gunpowder magazine, along with the Propylaea.
— The Erechtheion is transformed to a building for the harem of the Turk Garrison Commander.
1656 A.D. The blowing-up of the Propylaea from an explosion caused when lightning struck the magazine.
1687 A.D. Demolition of the temple of Nike, by the Turks and subsequent use of the building material for the construction of the wall, between the Pinacotheca and the Tower of the temple of Nike.
— Blowing-up and destruction of the Parthenon by Morozini's artillery and by the explosion of the gunpowder magazine which followed.
— Temporary occupation of the Acropolis by Morozini, and attempts made by him to dislodge sculptures of the Parthenon.
1799 - 1802/1803 A.D. Dislodgement and gradual removal to London, of a multitude of pieces of art and monuments of the Acropolis (the "Elginian marbles" of the British Museum). Lord Elgin, at the time, was ambassador of Great Britain to Constantinople, and the looting of these antiquities was accomplished with the permission of the Sultan.

RECENT TIMES

1822 A.D. (June 9) Occupation of the Acropolis by the Greek chieftain Odysseus Androutsos. Installation of a Greek guard on the Acropolis.
1827 A.D. A turkish shell destroys a part of the southern wall of the Erechtheion and causes damages to the Portico of the Korae (January).
— Re-occupation of the Acropolis by the Turks (March).
1833 A.D. Departure of the Turkish guard from the Acropolis. The first steps are taken for the restoration of the area and the monuments.
1834 A.D. King Otto proposes the building of the royal palace on the Acropolis, according to the designs of the architect Cleanthes.
1841 A.D. Restoration work on the Parthenon.
1846 A.D. Restoration work on the Portico of the Korae of the Erechtheion.
1852 A.D. Research and restoration of the so-called Beulé gate.
1874 A.D. Demolition of the medieval tower of "Koulas".
1885 - 1890 A.D. Systematic and extended excavation of the monuments of the Acropolis, done by the Archaeological Society.
1896 - 1900 A.D. Second phase of restoratory work on the Acropolis.
1902 - 1909 A.D. Important restoratory work of the Erechtheion.
1909 - 1917 A.D. Restoration of the Propylaea.
1922 - 1933 A.D. Extensive restoratory work on the Parthenon.
1935-1939. Demolition of the tower and the temple of Nike. Excavation of the interior of the tower and recovery of significant older traces. New restoration and reconstruction of the temple.
1959 A.D. Shaping of the ascent to the Acropolis.
1976 A.D. Formation of a committee of Greek scholars and specialists for the study of the deterioration of the marbles of the Acropolis from the pollution of the environment, and the measures that ought to be taken for their protection (UNESCO).

THE ACROPOLIS

The "Acropolis", the "Polis", the "Asty"

At the end of the 6th century B.C., the Athenians called the sacred rock "Acropolis" (high city) as opposed to the low city, "the asty" (the city), which was originally located outside the walled-in boundary of the region of the rock, where the populace lived.

When the institution of royalty fell (7th century B.C.) and the rule was taken over by the "eupatridae" (aristocrats), for a while, the Acropolis continued being the center of the city's public functions. When, however, the Athenian Democracy established itself, the center of the political, administrative, and judicial power was transferred to the Agora and the Pnyx. In so doing, the city grew and flourished outside the limits of the rock and the Acropolis which even in the 4th century B.C., kept the name "polis", remained exclusively the locale of shrines and worship.

The Rock and the Wall of the Acropolis

The venerable rock of the Acropolis "μεγαλόπετρος Παλλάδος ὄχθος" (big-rocked hill of Pallas), according to an ancient source (Arist.-Lys. 482), where Athena put up her shrine and where all humanity bows in pious adoration before the greatness of man's creation, is a creation which, combined with the ruggedness of landscape, dominates the entire region from a height of approximately 60 / 70 meters (156 meters above sea level). With the exclusion of the western, the other sides of the rock are steep, sheer and precipitous, while at the top, the level area has a length of 300 meters at its east-west, and of 150 meters at its north-south axis. The western slope is smoother, making the approach to the top accessible and having always been the main access to it.

The existence of springs of water on the slopes, decisively favored habitation and the use of the land by man, while the unapproachable height of the rock made it secure and offered assurance in times of danger. On the other hand, the shape and appearance of the rock led to the use of its surface area mainly, and the most extended level part of the southern side of the rock.

The wall which one has before him when looking at the Acropolis, is its fortification, as this was shaped during the first half of the 5th century B.C., after the Persian Wars. The final form we see today, however, was shaped during medieval times and the years of the Turkish occupation, when the various destructions that the wall had undergone were repaired, and later on, when restoration work was done, as well.

The earliest fortification of the rock took place during Mycenaean times in the second half of the 13th century B.C. The Mycenaean wall surrounds the rock, following the irregular, natural high contours, enclosing within it the Mycenaean palace and the entire settlement.

The "Cyclopean" wall had two entrances on the northern side, and another, the main one, at the south-west end of the rock, at the location where later on the Propylaea were built. Notable parts of the Cyclopean wall have been saved in quite a few places. We have ruins, which are now to be found deep inside the temple of Nike, and belong to the Mycenaean rampart, which had been built on a natural projection of the rock. Significant sections of the south wall can be seen to the south of the Propylaea, to the east of the temple of Nike, at the southwest corner of the Parthenon, to the east of the Museum of the Acropolis, to the east of the Erechtheion, and very few, on the north slope of the hill.

The fortification of the Acropolis was completed later on with the "Pelargic" wall, which, having been built at the north-west foot of the hill, enclosed the area from the Propylaea to the height of the building of the "Arrephoroi", including the fountain of the Clepsydra, and the three caves to the east.

During the years that followed, the so-called Sub-mycenaean and the Geometric periods, the western slope of the Acropolis was fortified with successive enclosures, among which the winding road, which led high up to the entrance of the Mycenaean wall, passed. These fortified enclosures, a continuation of the Pelargic wall, were certainly extended to the south slope of the hill, most probably to the boundary of what later was to be the Asklepieion, a fact which must have taken place during the Archaic period. These enclosures, with nine entrances in various places, are known as the "enneapylon" (nine-gates fortress).

The Mycenean wall, the Pelargic and the enneapylon were preserved in good condition until the years of Peisistratos and his son Hippias.

According to tradition, until 682 B.C., when royalty was abolished, the kings of Athens lived on the Acropolis, safe within its walls. Later on, when Peisistratos and his sons settled there, and the Acropolis was used as the "archon's" home, the wall was restored and a beautiful "propylon" (a very simple building of the propylaeum type) was built at its entrance. In 510 B.C., when Hippias was besieged by the Athenians within the walls of the Acropolis and then banished, the Athenians tore down and demolished the greatest part of the Mycenaean wall so that no other tyrant might fortify himself in it again. Thus, during the Persian Wars the Medes literally found the Acropolis unfortified. A year later, however (479 B.C.) Themistocles built a wall on the northern slope (Themistocles' wall) and then 12 years later (467 B.C.), Kimon completed the fortification of the wall of the southern slope (Kimon's wall). Kimon built it with the money he collected from the sale of the spoils of Eurymedon.

This fortification, which was done following the Persian Wars, did not follow the irregular course of the mycenaean fortification, but, while enclosing it, extended outward, with regular angles, extensive alignments, and huge piles of banking-up with earth on the inside. Much later, during the 3rd century A.D., the area was fortified to the west of the Propylaea, with a make-shift wall, built with the material of older monuments. This fortification was completed after the invasion of the Heroulians (267 A.D.), had two towers and two gates, one of which — the so-called Beulé gate — is the present entrance to the Acropolis.

The Way of the Panathenaia
The Street of the Tripods
The Peripatos of the Acropolis

Two roads led to the Acropolis, the "Way of the Panathenaia", and the "Street of the Tripods"(Plan at the end of the text). The Way of the Panathenaia owes its name to the most brilliant festival of Athens, the Panathenaia. This Way was followed by the multitude of the sacred procession of the Panathenaia, with equestrians, and the priestesses of Athena, who held the veil with which they were to clothe the cult statue in the Erechtheion, in the vanguard.

This road was well paved, giving access to pedestrians as well as chariots, and

Reconstruction of the monuments of the Acropolis (model by G. Stevens and J. Travlos).

started at the "Dipylon" of Cerameicos, passed the Basileios Stoa, the grounds where the altar of the twelve gods stood, between the Odeum of the Agora and the Stoa of Attalos, then continued in front of the Library of Pantaenos, and, finally, following the upward slope, terminated in front of the Clepsydra. The Panathenaic Way met the "Peripatos" of the Acropolis at this point.

The second road, the Street of the Tripods, which owes its name to the numerous choragic monuments with tripods, which had been placed all along its length, was one of the liveliest and busiest streets in ancient Athens, and the shortest route from the center of the Agora to the theater of Dionysos.

The Street of the Tripods which started at the "Prytaneum" (the senate committee building and some times the state dining-room in a greek city) followed the north and east foot of the Acropolis, then, turning south, and passing by the Odeum of Pericles, terminated at the theater of Dionysos.

One of the most picturesque and best preserved choragic monuments, which may still be seen at the Street of the Tripods, is the monument of Lysicrates (Plan, no **1**), which had been built by the "choragos" Lysicrates after his choral victory in the theater, in 334 B.C. The monument rested on a high, square podium of limestone, with a three-stepped "krepidoma". It is cylindrical, with the Greek corinthian capital still at the top, a capital with a three-sided form, to accommodate and support a bronze tripod.

View of the monuments of the Acropolis from the hill of Philopappos.

Six small semi-detached corinthian columns, of a 3.55 meter height, are attached to the cylindrical trunk of the monument, which is surmounted by a circular entablature with an architrave and a frieze. Reliefs, depicting scenes from the life of Dionysos, have been sculptured on the frieze.

The third road, directly connected with the Acropolis, and surrounding it peripherically, was the Peripatos. The Peripatos wound at a higher level, exactly below the

steep rocks of the hill, at the northern and southern slope. Passing by the north-east end of the Acropolis, the road terminated at the Odeion of Pericles and the theater of Dionysos. From the theater of Dionysos one reached the front of the Asklepieion and the Odeion of Herodes Atticos, along the north side of the Stoa of Eumenes. The expert on Athenian city-planning, the scholar John Travlos, has calculated the circumference of the road as being 1.100 meters long.

MONUMENTS AND SANCTUARIES OF THE SOUTHERN
SLOPE OF THE ACROPOLIS

The Sanctuary of Dionysos Eleuthereus

The sanctuary of the god is located at the south side of the theater of Dionysos (Plan, nos **3,4,5,6**). This is one of the three most significant shrines of Dionysos, having been characterized by Pausanias as a "most ancient shrine". The sanctuary has two entrances, one towards the east and another towards the west. In the south, it is surrounded by the circuitous ancient "street of the Tripods", and includes two small temples of Dionysos Eleuthereus, an earlier (no **3**) and a more recent one (no **4**), and an altar (no **5**). A long stoa is located in the north (no **6**), its rear wall serving as the boundary of the stage of the theater of Dionysos, with which it has a definite functional relationship. The smaller of the two temples, which is attached to the west end of the stoa, was built by the Peisistratides at approximately 540 B.C., and housed the "xoanon" (crude primitive wooden idol) of the god. According to tradition, this xoanon had been brought from Eleutherae of Boeotia by Pegasos, a priest of the god. This temple, with dimensions of 13.50× 8 meters, had an entrance facing the east. It is a temple in antis and was still in existence during Pausanias' time.

The other temple, with dimensions of 21.95× 10.5 meters, a prostyle, was larger than the former one, had been built in the 4th century B.C., and housed the chryselephantine (gold and ivory) statue of Dionysos, the work of the sculptor Alcamenes. This temple has the same orientation as the older one, is parallel and close to it, being located just to the south.

Pausanias refers to both temples and to the statues housed in each one. We may only see their foundations now, while ruins of the stoa and the altar are still extant at present.

The Theater of Dionysos Eleuthereus

The theater of Dionysos Eleuthereus is directly associated with the connected sacred shrine of the god, literally constituting its organic and functional extension (Plan, nos **7,8**).

Sometime during the middle of the 6th century B.C., when the xoanon of Dionysos was transported from Eleutherae and housed in the earlier temple of the god, that is, long before the building of the theater as we know it today, a religious festival of a circular dithyrambic choral dancing by masked men, disguised as goats, was instituted.

In order to perform the dithyrambic choral dance, a circular area of approximately 25 meters in diameter was leveled. This area was located near the earlier temple, at a higher level, at the exact site of the orchestra of the existing theater (no **8**). The natural rocky formation of the adjoining slope of the hill was used by the citizens during the performances of the dance.

This dance-cult of Dionysos Eleuthereus constitutes the most primitive expression and is the origin of the ancient greek drama.

The new form of the theater of Dionysos on the slopes of the Acropolis developed and took shape in stages, which followed the evolution of the drama in Athens and the introduction of drama contests during the "greater Dionysia".

In this manner, in the middle of the 5th century B.C., most probably following the Persian Wars, the site of the theater of Dionysos presented the following arrangement: The circular area, that had been leveled approximately a century earlier, now has a 20-meter diameter of stamped earth, and is surrounded by a drainage channel. For the comfort of the spectators, wooden bleachers were erected on the slope overlooking the orchestra, and the foundations of a simple wooden skene were laid; the latter being a necessity for the immediate appearance and performance of the actors. The wooden "skene" (no **7**) was built along the back of the rectangular stoa which was located in the sanctuary, between the earlier temple of Dionysos Eleuthereus and the area leveled for the performance of the dithyrambic choral dances.

The plays of the three great tragedians, Aischylos, Sophocles, and Euripides, and of Aristophanes, the writer of comedy, were performed in a theater of this form.

Since it is immediately connected with the action (dromena) of the drama, the structure of the skene is considered the most significant element in the study of the development of the history of the theater.

This latter tripartite arrangement of the theater of Dionysos — orchestra, cavea (auditorium), skene — is the final product of an interrelated succession of expressions, acts, and solutions, in other words, of a process which contains the following basic elements:

a) The lofty human message of the Dionysiac cult.

b) The conception and religious character of the dithyrambic choral dancing, with its masked actors in the chosen site within the sacred sanctuary of the god.

c) The confrontation of purely practical solutions, which were demanded by the spectacle, as it was related to the spectators and the conditions of the site.

d) Finally, the gradual estrangement of the tragedy from the cult of the god, and its influence upon the aesthetic beliefs and demands of the times.

The changes, re-arrangements, and various interventions in the plan of the theater start at the beginning of the 5th century and continue until the 3rd century B.C. The greatest number and the most decisive changes were made in the skene, which was a simple wooden structure in the 5th century B.C., but in the 4th century B.C. was composed of a large rectangular building, the main skene, which was 49.5× 8 meters in dimensions, with two square areas at the two ends, the "paraskenia" or symmetrical wings of the skene, and with the "proskenion" in front, which aided the entrance of the actors. The skene was built for the first time during the era of the Peace of Nikias, 421 - 415 B.C.

Following the form they had acquired by the 6th century B.C., the orchestra and the cavea did not undergo many organically decisive changes.

The year 330 B.C. is a significant milestone in the history and the evolution of theater of Dionysos. At that time, when Lycourgos was archon in Athens, practically all the wooden benches were substituted with stone stands and the cavea acquired its final form, while simultaneously a special enclosure was built around the sanctuary of Dionysos, separating and organically alienating the shrine of the god from the theater. Of the great tragedians, only Menandros presented his plays in the marble theater which held 16,000 spectators.

During Nero's time, the theater was dedicated to the emperor. Its skene was renovated at that time, becoming a building of two storeys, while the orchestra was paved with marble.

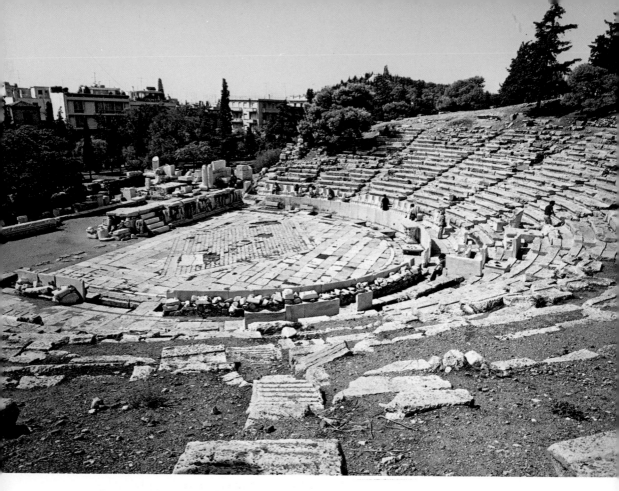

Present condition of the theater of Dionysos.

Later on, during the era of the roman emperors, the orchestra was transformed into an arena for the games of gladiators.

In 270 A.D., three years after the destruction of the monuments of Athens by the Heroulians, Phaedros the archon of Athens, repaired the theater and renovated its skene. During the early Christian era a three-aisled basilica was built on the site of the theater of Dionysos.

Extant today we may see the paved orchestra in its latter semi-circular shape, a part of the proskenion with sculptured decorations, foundations, and a few parts of the stone structure of the skene. One may also see the lower part of the cavea with marble thrones, and seats with honorary inscriptions, on the three front rows which were reserved for the priests, archons, and benefactors of the demos.

As a conception, form, and architectural solution, the theater of Dionysos is the prototype, and, at the same time, the fore-runner of the spirit of the theater as it has evolved from antiquity to the present day.

The Odeion of Pericles

The "Odeion" (music hall) of Pericles, an immense four-sided hypostylon hall, with dimensions of 62.40× 68.60 meters, is located adjacent to the eastern end of the theater of Dionysos (Plan, no **2**). The Odeion is directly related to the theater, having an odd topographical relation to it, jutting into it, so to speak, where the N.W. angle of the Odeion thrusts itself into the theater, displacing part of the second diazoma (upper rows) of the cavea. However, in reality the opposite is true. The extension of the cavea of the theater in the 4th century was stopped by the existence of the Odeion, which had already been there since the 5th century B.C., thus forcing the former to a structural accommodation.

The excavation of the Odeion has been confined to the discovery of parts of its foundations only. Besides a northern entrance, the Odeion most probably had entrances on all remaining three sides. In the interior, three rows of columns supported all four sides of the hall, leaving an open space in the middle, which was meant to be used by the musicians. The columns (72 in all) with architraves, and additional rows of columns over these, held up an extremely high pyramidal roof, whose form caused Pausanias to exclaim that it was a creation "in imitation of Xerxes' tent".

The Odeion, which had been the inspiration and was built under the supervision of Pericles himself, held wooden stands for the seating of the spectators, and was meant to be used for the performance of all musical programs and contests, including those of the Panathenaic games.

The Odeion was built in 445 B.C., was burned to the ground by the Athenians themselves just before Sulla's invasion of the city in 86 B.C., and was restored in 61 B.C. by Ariobarzanes the Second, the king of Cappadocia.

The Choragic Monument of Thrasyllos

According to the inscription on the architrave of the monument (Plan, no 9), it was built in 319 B.C., after the choragic victory of Thrasyllos, at the time when Neaichmos was archon of Athens. A small cavern, which is located above and behind the theater of Dionysos, was used for this purpose. The natural depression of the rock was hewn out to meet the specifications of the monument, thus creating an area of 6.20× 1.70 meters and a height of approximately 6 meters. The rectangular opening was framed by two marble piers on each side. These two, a third central pier, an entablature, and two large marble portals closed the opening. The choragic tripod was placed over the entablature on a pedestal with three steps. Approximately forty years later, in 270 B.C., when Thrasyllos' son Thrasykles won two victories as "agonothetes" (judge of the contests, president of the ancient greek Games or, later, exhibitor of the Games), he added two more tripods to the right and left of his father's central tripod. Their pedestals and votive inscriptions are still visible today. Pausanias, who most certainly must have seen this monument sometime around 150 A.D., makes no reference to it. It is obvious, however, that he does refer to its interior when he mentions the representation of Apollo and Artemis killing Niobe's children. It is not clear, however, whether the tripod mentioned by Pausanias (as still standing over the cavern) belongs to the monument of Thrasyllos or to one of the other two choragic columns that stand higher up on the rock, above this monument.

After 200 A.D. it seems that the function and form of the monument changed, and that in place of the three tripods an equal number of statues was set up. It is characteristic that in the middle of the 18th century, in 1761, the English architects Stuart and Revett sketched the monument with the statue of a seated female figure in place of the central tripod. Much later than the 3rd century A.D., and before the 18th, the cavern was changed to a christian church, dedicated to Panagia Spiliotissa (The Virgin Mary of the cave).

Choragic Columns above the Monument of Thrasyllos

Two unfluted marble columns — practically equal in size — carrying three-sided corinthian capitals, stand tall above the natural solid rocky ceiling of the monument of Thrasyllos (Plan, no **10**). The triangular shape of the two capitals show how the columns were used specifically to support an equal number of choragic tripods. The columns are dated in the Roman era, but the incidents associated with their dedication are unknown to us.

Choragic Monument of Nikias

According to the inscription on its architrave, this monument was built in 319 B.C., when Neaichmos was archon in Athens, following the choragic victory of Nikias, son of Nikodemos (Plan, no **11**).

The architectural style of this monument, with dimensions of 16.68× 11.79 meters, is that of a "prostyle temple", with six doric columns, and an entrance towards the west. The rear wall of the monument is located less than 15 meters away from the western end of the cavea of the theater of Dionysos. The importance and brilliance of the monument in antiquity are attested by the fact that, 150 years later, the architect of the

Facade of the choragic monument of Thrasyllos (by G. Welter).

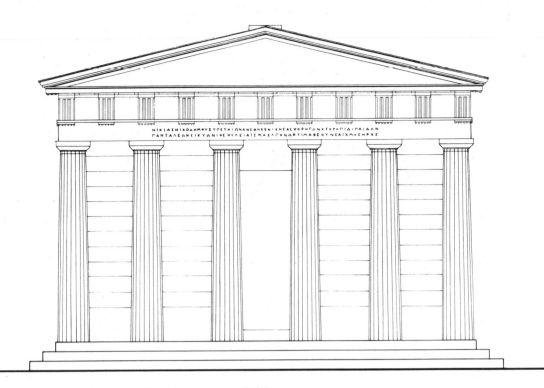

Reconstruction of the western side of the monument of Nikias.

Stoa of Eumenes respected it and cleverly connected it with the latter, creating a right angle with the stoa's colonnade and the facade of the choragic monument.

Today, the foundation is the only visible part of the monument of Nikias. The most significant architectural members of the superstructure, such as pilasters, architraves, triglyphs, metopes and cornices were used as building material and were immured in the towers of the Beulé gate, when the Athenians demolished the monument and hurriedly built the fortifications of the Acropolis, after the invasion of the Heroulians in 267 A.D. Pausanias makes no mention of this monument.

The Shrine of Asklepios

The shrine of Asklepios (Plan, nos **12 - 17**) is adjoined to the N.W. end of the cavea of the theater of Dionysos, and is located between the "Peripatos" and the steep perpendicular rocks of the southern slope of the Acropolis. A spring flows from a depression in the rock, this being an indispensable element in the establishment and functioning of an Asklepieion.

The Asklepieion, which was founded by a certain Telemachos of Acharnai after 420 B.C., when the cult of the god was introduced to Athens, consists of a group of structures which are:

a) The temple of the god (no **12**), with dimensions of 10.40× 6 meters, a simple cella, a tetrastyle facade in the east with an altar (no **13**) in front of it, while the statues of Asklepios and Hygieia stood on a pedestal at the far end of the cella.

b) A stoa, with two storeys (no **14**), and dimensions of 49.90× 9.75 meters, served as "enkoimeterion", that is, a temporary refuge (dormitory) of the patients and was located to the north of the temple. The stoa had an interior ionic colonnade and 17 doric columns in the front (original style), while in the back the northern wall had an

The cave where the monument of Thrasyllos used to be; two extant choragic columns above it.

opening which led to a circular hand-hewn cave-like area, out of which flowed a spring of water. Today, this cave is a chapel which, during the early-christian era became an addition, probably a baptistery, to the large three-aisled basilica, that had taken over the entire site of the Asklepieion.

c) A square room (no **15**), with a southern entrance, was located at the north-west end of the stoa and had a circular "Bothros" (sacrificial pit) of a 2.70 meter diameter and a depth of 2.20 meters, into which the sacred remains of sacrifices were thrown.

d) An oblong structure, the so-called ionic stoa (no **17**), was located to the west of the square room, whose dimensions were 28× 14 meters, had 4 adjoining rooms at the far end, and in the front a stoa with an ionic colonnade. This structure which had been built later than the temple and the two-storey stoa, was used as an enkoimeterion, or dormitory for the patients.

e) Finally, a stoa, which was open towards the temple of Asklepios (no **16**), was added during the Roman era, and had a rear wall which ran all along the southern side of the sanctuary.

The Asklepieion had an entrance with a propylon to the west of the roman stoa, exactly at the boundary of the Peripatos.

20

The Fountain of Alkippe, the Temple of Themis and the "Hippolyteion"

A spring, which even during the Archaic age had already been shaped into a fountain (Plan, no **18**), is located to the west of the ionic stoa of the Asklepieion. Today, one may see a square-shaped well of an approximate depth of 3 meters, and sides measuring 3× 2.70 meters. This well, built of polygonal masonry, constitutes the basin of the fountain. It is most probable that the fountain was dedicated to the nymph Alkippe, a fact which is in harmony with the known traditional cult of the nymphs on this slope of the Acropolis. When the Asklepieion was founded, the archaic fountain had already been in use for some time. A tile-covered cistern, which is attached to the fountain is found next to it, while further to the south there is still another cistern, both having been built during medieval times.

The small temple-shaped building (Plan, no **19**), which is located to the south of the archaic fountain, with dimensions of 5.06× 4.25 meters, was probably a temple dedicated to the goddess Themis.

Tradition places the "Hippolyteion" (shrine dedicated to Hippolytos, son of Theseus), and the shrine of "Aphrodite on Hippolytos" («ἐφ' Ἱππολύτῳ Ἀφροδίτη») (Plan, no **20**), to the west of the small temple of Themis, probably somewhere near the medieval cisterns. At any rate, the hero's tomb and the shrine had already been built before the Asklepieion was founded on the same site.

The Stoa of Eumenes

An extremely long two-storey building (163 meters long by 17.68 meters wide), the "Stoa of Eumenes" (Plan, no **21**), a gift of the king of Pergamum Eumenes the Second to the city of Athens, was constructed during the first half of the 2nd century B.C. Its purpose was to serve the numerous spectators of the theater of Dionysos, and is located to the west of its cavea, having its rear wall on the boundary of the Peripatos.

Due to a difference in the height of the level of the ground, the foundations of the stoa may be found at a much lower level than that of the Peripatos. This necessitated the construction of a retaining wall, which had a row of arches on its upper part, before the northern wall of the stoa could be built. Communication from the ground floor to the upper storey and the level of the Peripatos was attained by a staircase, which had been built along the eastern narrow side of the stoa, exactly to the north of the choragic monument of Nikias.

Most probably the stoa had an ionic colonnade, which probably consisted of 32 columns in the interior and, respectively, in the front, a doric colonnade of 64 columns.

The Stoa of Eumenes the Second, which was originally a building that was functionally tied with the theater of Dionysos and later on with the Odeion of Herodes Atticos, occupied and embellished the entire area between these two structures.

The Odeion of Herodes Atticos

The "Odeion of Herodes Atticos" (Plan, no **22**) is situated at the western end of the southern slope of the Acropolis, and is the last of the large imposing public edifices that were built in this area which, for centuries, had been dedicated to the service of music and dramatic art.

The building of the Odeion began in 160/161 A.D. by the famous orator, sophist and consul of Rome, Herodes Atticos. It had been built in memory of his wife, Regilla, who had died that same year, and was meant to be used for artistic and, generally, other cultural demonstrations. Herodes, who was born in 101 A.D. in Marathon of Attica, had inherited a fabulous wealth, which he disposed of in the construction of many public buildings, not only in Attica but in other parts of Greece, as well, and can justifiably be considered the Maecenas of his time. The Odeion, for which an immense amount of money was spent, was probably the last big offer of the donor to Athens, and, at the same time a famous ornament of the city, until its destruction by the invasion of the Heroulians in 267 A.D.

As a contrast to its neighboring Odeion of Pericles, the Odeion of Herodes had been built as an amphitheater, following the established and typical architectural style of the theater of the imperial age. The cavea of the Odeion has a diameter of 75 meters, and its semi-circular orchestra one of 19 meters. The skene of the theater was three storeys high and contained a "logeion" (literally speaking place), as well. The length of the skene was 92 meters, and its height at the facade was approximately 28 meters. The height of the logeion was 1.10 meters.

It is highly possible that the Odeion had been roofed in its entirety, even over its cavea. Cedar wood had been used for its roof, and its whole construction had been luxurious. The walls had been lined with marble, and the same material had been used for the architectural details of the structure and sculptured embellishment of the skene, for the columns of the proskenium in front of the decorative niches, and for the construction of the seats of the cavea.

The cavea of the Odeion had been divided by a "diazoma" half-way up the amphitheater, in a manner that allowed five sections of 20 rows each below, and 10 sections of 14 rows each above, permitting the seating of approximately 6000 spectators.

It seems that originally the access and entrance to the theater was made from the east, that is, from the ground floor of the Stoa of Eumenes and from its upper storey which was used in a way that led directly to the diazoma of the cavea. Recent excavations have revealed that later on changes were made, and the main access to the Odeion was from the south, that is, from the facade of the building.

The structural relation and the continued uninterrupted functional relation of the Odeion to the Stoa of Eumenes have given the impression that the Stoa had not been built for the theater of Dionysos, but for the Odeion of Herodes Atticos which was actually constructed three centuries later.

The Odeion, which is known today as the "Herodeion", having undergone restoratory work and having been provided with marble seats for its cavea, is used for the performances of ancient greek drama and for musical recitals and concerts.

SHRINES ON THE SOUTHWESTERN END OF THE ACROPOLIS

The shrine of "Pandemos Aphrodite", whose worship, according to evidence from recent excavations, took place at the western end of the Acropolis, and had already been established by the end of the 6th century B.C., was located on the level area which is to be found exactly under the foundation upon which the temple of Nike rests. Carvings, visible on the grounds and used in the foundation of the small temple, sculptured niches on the surface of he perpendicular rock, and an inscribed marble architrave confirm the existence of the temple of Aphrodite, who is named, or called on the inscription ''..... the great, respected Aphrodite''. As Pausanias reports, Pandemos Aphrodite was worshipped by the Athenians with great honors; statues by famous artists offered to her shrine, were to be found there.

Literary sources and evidence from inscriptions confirm that the area under the Propylaea, near the shrine of Pandemos, must have been dedicated to the shrine of Blaute and the common sanctuary of Gaia Kourotrophos, and Demeter Chloe, each with its own altar (Plan, no **25**).

SHRINES ON THE NORTHERN SLOPE OF THE ACROPOLIS

Clepsydra

The water fountain of ''Clepsydra'' (the former name of the spring was Empedo) is located at the western end of the Acropolis, farther to the north of the monument of Agrippa, in a small natural cavern, at the exact spot where the last section of the Panathenaic route terminated (Plan, no **26**). Nymphs were worshipped in this and other caves, in which water was to be found. In the 5th century B.C. the spring was fashioned into a structure with dimensions of 7.80× 6.70 meters, a rectangular basin (4.50× 2.23) was carved in the rock, while a paved court (18× 9 meters) surrounded the fountain at its northern and eastern sides.

In the third century A.D., most probably after the invasion of the Heroulians, at the same time when the area below the Propylaea was being fashioned and re-arranged, a staircase of 69 steps descending towards the Clepsydra was built. This descent originates at the northern side of the monument of Agrippa, and passes underneath the wall.

A church, dedicated to the Holy Apostles, was built on the site of the Clepsydra during medieval times. The spring of water, which by then had become a well, was enclosed within the church.

The Shrines of Apollo, Zeus, and Pan

Three small sacred caves, which are located near the Clepsydra were dedicated to an equivalent number of gods. The cave which is closest to the cave of the Clepsydra, the so-called ''Pythion'' must have been the shrine of Apollo (Plan, no **27**) where, according to legend, the god slept with the beautiful daughter of Erechtheus, Kreousa. Pausanias calls this sanctuary of the god ''Apollo 's shrine in the cave''.

Olympian Zeus was worshipped in the ''Olympion'' (Plan, no **28**), the second cave, while in the third cave (Plan, no **29**), as well as in other neighboring depressions in the rock, Pan and the Nymphs were probably worshipped, even as early as the beginning of the 5th century B.C.

The Shrine of Aphrodite and Eros

The site of the shrine of Aphrodite and Eros has been fixed at the northern foot of the rock, exactly under the northeastern border of the Erechtheion, near the mycenaean

The Odeion of Herodes Atticos.

staircase (Plan, no **30**). This was closely related to the apocryphal rituals of the "Arre-phoroi" who, for this purpose, communicated with their house (oikos) on the Acropolis through a secret passage.

The Aglaureion

Pausanias refers to yet one more shrine whose location has been fixed to the west of the shrine of Aphrodite, this being the "Aglaureion", dedicated to the worship of Aglauros, the daughter of Cecrops (Plan, no **31**). The young men of Athens used to go to the Aglaureion and vow that they would defend their land, and not bring shame to their arms.

The Anakeion

The shrine dedicated to the Dioscouroi, Castor and Polydeukes, the "Anakeion" is also located at the foot of the rock, to the south of the Aglaureion (Plan, no **32**).

THE WESTERN END OF THE ACROPOLIS

The Access to the Sacred Rock

The western end of the Acropolis, narrow, sloping, and rocky, but by its nature, accessible, as well, was the only suitable and unimpeded access to the rock. These are

The ascent to the Acropolis from the west.

the reasons that this approach, from the foot of the hill to the spot where higher up the surface of the rock becomes smoother and levels off, was used continuously, underwent many and various changes and took many forms through the centuries.

During Neolithic times, as well as during the entire Prehistoric era, a path must have been used, which followed the natural contours and formation of the land, and led to the top of the hill. During Mycenaean times, before and after the building of fortifications on the rock, it is certain that a wider, spiral road had substituted the prehistoric path, and, most probably, work must have been done to facilitate the ascent, the latter presupposing the existence of a palace, and a larger settlement on the hill.

For reasons of defence, the first serious interference at the area of the access to the rock, took place during the Sub-mycenaean and Geometric era, terminating later on at the enneapylon. A spiral, uphill road developed, a road which was shaped by buttressed walls, with a large number of successive gates and, most probably, was protected by defensive bastions. This road terminated at the cyclopean propylon of the Acropolis. The form that the entrance to the Acropolis had taken, as described so far, included altars and small shrines, dedicated to gods and heroes, and was preserved until the re-organization of the Panathenaic festival in 566 B.C., when a new monumental entrance was built, one which could accommodate an unimpeded movement of the crowds that participated in the Panathenaic procession. This entrance also had buttressed, oblique walls of poros limestone, created a straight, sloping plane of a 10 meter width by an approximate length of 80 meters, which originated at the foot of the hill and terminated at the entrance of the Acropolis, where, it is possible that, during that time, a monumental "propylon", worthy of the Acropolis, had been erected. A part of the northern buttressed wall of this access, constructed in a "polygonal" manner, may be seen to the east of the Beulé gate.

This monumental entrance to the Acropolis preserved its form until 437 - 432 B.C., when the Propylaea were built, according to Mnesicles' plans. It was then that the width of the access doubled, in order to accommodate the demands of the new plan. We may get a fairly good idea of the picture this entrance presented from the remnants of sections of the northern, oblique, buttressed wall which may be seen to the east of the northern tower of the Beulé gate, as well as, the opposite wall, to the south, where one sees the chiselled, sloping, natural rock.

The wide entrance of Mnesicles remained unaltered until the middle of the 1st century A.D. During the last years of the reign of emperor Claudius, a monumental marble staircase was constructed, which covered practically the entire width of the sloping plane, exactly at the plane below the Propylaea.

Extant, practically in their entire length, we have today four steps of the original marble staircase, which is located exactly on the inside of the Beulé gate.

After the Archaeological Society was founded in 1837, a new, narrower staircase, on the side of the Tower of Nike, was built with material gathered from other steps of this staircase, and led on to the Propylaea (Pittaki staircase).

The original form of the sloping access to the Acropolis no longer exists, since the Beulé fortification, with its two towers and the gate between them, radically changed the ancient picture and appearance of this entrance.

The Altar of Apollo Agyieus

At the entrance to the Acropolis, to the east of the Beulé gate, next to the polygonal wall, one finds a poros archaic altar (Plan, no **34**). From an inscription of the imperial age, which was found nearby and which speaks of another altar dedicated by the guardians of the gates to the Acropolis, to Apollo Agyieus, one assumes that the god was worshipped under the epithet ''Agyieus'' at this specific location, and was the protector of the entrance and roads.

The Shrine of Athena Pylatis

Directly associated with the entrance to the Acropolis, one finds the double-niched shrine of Athena Pylatis, which is located in the western side of the tower of Athena Nike (Plan, no **35**). The visitor, today, may see this shrine upon entering, to the right of the Beulé gate. In antiquity, the pilgrim left his votive offerings to the goddess here, making his first pilgrimage, so to speak, to the sacred rock, before ascending to the top. Athena Pylatis was the protectress and guardian of the entrance to the entire sacred rock.

The shrine of Athena Pylatis was recovered after the demolition and restoration of the tower of the temple of Nike, just before the Second World War.

The Pedestal of Eumenes — The Quadriga of Agrippas

In the area of the entrance, under the southwest angle of the northern wing of the Propylaea, and practically at the same height the tower of the temple of Nike, one finds an extremely tall pedestal of bluish marble, of a height of 13.40 meters. Its foundation is 4.50 meters tall, with sides of 3.30 × 3.80 meters (Plan, no **36**). The bronze quadriga of the king of Pergamum, Eumenes the Second, stood on this pedestal. The king, himself, and his brother Attalos were the riders and victors of the Panathenaic games of 178 B.C.

Around 27 B.C., the quadriga of Eumenes the Second, was substituted by another bronze quadriga of Agrippas, as the votive inscription, which may be seen on the western side of the pedestal, shows.

As a consequence, this monument is known as the pedestal of Agrippas. We know of the fact that the quadriga of Eumenes stood there originally, through another inscription, whose traces may be vaguelly seen under the inscription of Agrippas.

THE MONUMENTS OF THE ACROPOLIS

The Propylaea

With their monumental construction, the Propylaea of the Acropolis are a structure of an importance comparable to that of the temples and shrines on the sacred rock (Plan, no **37**).

Built on the old late-archaic propylon, from the designs of the architect Mnesicles, the Propylaea are one of the structures belonging to Pericles' great scheme of embellishing the Acropolis.

Literary sources give us information concerning the plan of the edifice, the amount of money spent — 2.012 talants — the length of time devoted to its construction, that is, the period of 437 - 432 B.C. It seems, however, that the work was interrupted and never resumed, due to the Peloponnesian War.

The central area of the Propylaea, of a 25 meter length and a width of 8 meters, is defined by 6 doric columns each, on the two facades, at the east-west axis, and the two side walls on the axis of the outermost columns. At a distance of 10 meters, a cross-wall divides the eastern facade from the central area of the Propylaea, in two sections, the eastern one being on a higher level. This cross-wall has five openings of which the central, which was used for the entrance of the sacrificial animals, had a width of

Propylon of the Acropolis of Athens, about 488 to 437 B.C. (by G. Stevens).

approximately 4 meters, those on either side of the central colonnades had openings of approximately 3 meters, while the other two, the end ones, an opening of 1.5 meters.

The roof of the western section, which was at a lower level, on the one hand — in the interior — rested on two colonnades of three extremely tall ionic columns, of a 10.39 meter height, which were arranged along the length of the limits of the central opening, while on the other hand, it rested on the columns of the western facade, of a height of 8.81 meters, the columns of the eastern facade having a height of 8.53 meters.

The roofs at both facades terminated in pediments. Part of the entablature, along with the sima are extremely well preserved at the north-eastern corner of the eastern facade.

Artistically beautiful coffers, which were decorated, in the center with golden stars and numerous rays, had been carved on the ceilings of the central building of the Propylaea.

The Pinacotheca

Two symmetrical wings, with the facades opposite each other, the northern and southern ones, were created to the right and left of west tern facade of the Propylaea.

The northern wing consisted of a portico,which was shaped by a colonnade of three

The Periclean entrance court of the Acropolis of Athens (by G. Stevens).

The western facade of the Propylaea.

doric columns in antis, and one large hall (10.76× 8.97 meters) which had couches on all four sides, along the length of its walls. The southern wall of the hall had an entrance with windows on either side, looking outward at the portico. This large hall, the well-known "Pinacotheca" (Plan, no **38**) was intended for the exhibit of paintings (wooden ones), as well as, for the sojourn and rest of the visitors of the Acropolis.

We know from Pausanias that, in this hall, which he called "the building with the pictures" among other paintings, one found the famous composition of Polygnotos "Achilleus in Skyros". The southern wing of the Propylaea consisted only of a porch which was slightly wider than that of the northern wing. There is no chamber on the back side here, but in place of the western wall of the porch one finds, to the right and left of a central pier, large openings which offered a good view and an ascent to the temple of Nike.

A Building with two Chambers

Two adjoining chambers, with entrances to the south and back sides on the northern wall of the Acropolis, are to be found to the northeast of the "Pinacotheca" (Plan, no **39**). The purpose of this structure and the use to which it was put remain unknown.

The Temple of Nike

The little ionic "amphiprostyle" temple (with porticoes of columns in front and rear side only) of Athena Nike (Plan, no **40**), rises high on its tower-like pedestal, an elegant ornament and light complement of the Propylaea which are loaded down with heavy structures.

29

As has already been mentioned, the temple of Nike was built on a classical tower, which, in turn, had been built on the site of the prehistoric rampart on the naturally impregnable projection of the rock.

The temple rests on a four-stepped "krepidoma" with dimensions at the stylobate of 8.268× 5.64 meters, consists of a "cella" with dimensions of 3.78× 4.14, and has four ionic fluted monolithic columns of a 4.066-meter height at the short sides (east-west). The eastern side of the cella was open. Two piers between the antae (pilasters or corner posts of slight projection terminating the end of the lateral walls of a cella) formed the central entrance, 1.50 meters wide, with two rectangular openings closed in front by bronze screens between the piers and antae. The temple did not have a "pronaos" or "opisthodomos", but only a cella which housed the cult statue.

The architraves, with a tripartite horizontal ionic arrangement, rest on the two colonnades and the walls of the cella,while a continuous sculptured "zophoros", of 0.45 meters in height, encircles and crowns the temple.

The gods of Olympos were the subject of the sculptured embellishments of the zophoros, on the eastern side, while the other three sides depicted scenes of combat of the Greeks against barbarians, or even against greek allies of the Persians. Most of the sculptured parts of the zophoros are to be found in the British Museum, having been snatched up by Elgin. The sculptured representations of the eastern side are the only ones in their original position.

As it appears from the holes which can be seen on the horizontal cornice, the pediments of the temple had sculptured representations whose subject, or theme has remained unknown to us.

A marble "thorakion" (parapet) of a height of 1.50 meters, decorated with winged Victories in high relief, and graceful figures of Athena, had been sculptured over the steep sides of the Tower, on the three sides of the temple of Nike. The Victories, presented in many variations, usually lead animals to sacrifice, offer gifts to the goddess, or decorate a trophy. The sculptures of this thorakion, the work of Callimachos who was one of the most famous sculptors of the end of the 5th century B.C., may be seen at the Museum on the Acropolis. It seems that, for reasons of security, the thorakion was surmounted by an iron grille.

The stone altar of the goddess used to stand opposite the entrance of the temple. Only parts of its marble lining have been preserved.

The foundations of an earlier minuscule temple were found at the same site, under the foundations of the temple of Nike, at a depth of 1.40 meters. It had been built in the second quarter of the 6th century B.C. This temple, a simple rectangular cella with exterior dimensions of 2.31× 3.50 meters, had two poros altars in front of it, one of which has a votive inscription to Athena Nike on it.

Both temples, the archaic and classical one, had been dedicated to Athena Nike and not to the winged goddess Nike. This is the reason why Pausanias called the goddess who was worshipped at the temple "apteros Nike" (wingless Victory).

According to a decree of 449/448 B.C., it seems that the temple of Nike had been designed by the architect of the Parthenon, Callicrates. However, it was not built at once, due to lack of money, internal political strife (Pericles-Kimon's followers), and especially, due to the Peloponnesian War.

The temple was probably built in 427 B.C., in other words, two years after the death of Pericles,while the cult statue of the goddess,"xoanon apteron" (wingless wooden statue), with a helmet in the right hand and a pomegranate in the left, was completed

Reconstruction of the temple of Athena Nike.

two years later and the thorakion with the Victories much later, around 410 B.C., after the war victories of Alcibiades.

In 1687, the year that the Parthenon was destroyed, the temple of Nike was also dismembered by the Turks in order to be used as building material for the fortification wall, which was to secure the entrance to the Acropolis from an attack of the army of Morozini.

The temple of Nike was restored in the 19th century (after the founding of an independent Greek State) by the Germans Ross and Schaubert, and the Danish architect Hansen, after the various architectural members and part of the sculptured decorations, that had been immured in the Turkish wall, had been found and identified. Later on, due to the half-ruined, dangerous condition of the Tower the temple underwent a new total dismantling and restoration. This work was done by the Greek Department of Archaeology before the Second World War.

The Shrine of Brauronia Artemis

The foundation of a sanctuary, of the 5th century B.C., which was dedicated to the cult of Artemis Brauronia is located adjacent to, and to the southeast of the Propylaea (Plan, no **41**). The cult of the goddess, who protected women about to give birth, or women in confinement, had been transported earlier, during the time of Peisistratos, from Brauron of Attica to the Acropolis. According to mythology, Iphigeneia had brought the cult statue (xoanon) of the goddess from the land of Tauris.

This sanctuary, which is known from inscriptions as "Brauronion", — with an entrance at its northeast corner — had a long stoa, of a 38-meter length and a width of 7 meters, at the border all along the wall of Kimon, and a facade with a doric colonnade of

31

The Ionic temple of Athena Nike.

10 columns open to the north. Two chambers, 10×7 meters, each with a northern entrance, in other words at the center of the sanctuary, were located at the two ends of the stoa, and were used for the safe-keeping of valuable votive offerings to the goddess (treasuries).

Later on, a second stoa was added, an extension of the eastern chamber, having the same width as the older — the main stoa — but a shorter length of 17 meters.

The cult statue of the goddess, which was exactly the same in appearance as the xoanon of Brauron, stood in one of the two chambers of the stoa, but, according to Pausanias, there existed yet one more cult statue of the goddess, which had been sculptured by Praxiteles. Offerings stood in the courtyard, at the centre.

Pausanias refers to a large bronze horse, which stood on a marble pedestal, and was an effigy of the Trojan horse.

The Chalcotheca

The Chalcotheca, well-known from inscriptions, is adjacent to the Brauronion, to the east, and one may see the foundations of the oblong structure of the middle of the 5th century B.C. (Plan, no **42**). Its dimensions were 43 × 14 meters, and it had an interior colonnade for the support of the roof. Pausanias doesn't mention the building.

The south side of the structure was parallel to the wall of the Acropolis, the west bordered the Brauronion, and the north, with three openings, faced a stoa which was added later, at the beginning of the 4th century B.C. and which had a façade with a colonnade of 18 columns.

The northeast corner of the stoa has destroyed a section of the carved steps which carried one up to a higher level, at the western end of the Parthenon.

As we know from the evidence on inscriptions, various bronze articles, especially arms, as well as votive offerings, which were the property of the goddess Athena, were kept in the Chalcotheca.

The Parthenon

Within two centuries, three ancient greek temples were probably built on the same site on the Acropolis (Plan, no **43**), that is, at the exact spot where, from the middle of the 5th century B.C. to this day, the imposing and majestic Parthenon (Parthenon III), the third temple dedicated to the worship of the goddess Athena stands tall and commanding. Inscriptions, literary sources, and other direct, or indirect archaeological evidence refer to the two earlier Parthenons (Parthenon I and Parthenon II).

The Parthenon I

The Parthenon I, an archaic doric temple, was probably built on the Acropolis during the first quarter of the 6th century B.C. The building material used for the construction,

Sanctuary of the Brauronia Artemis on the Acropolis of Athens (by G. Stevens).

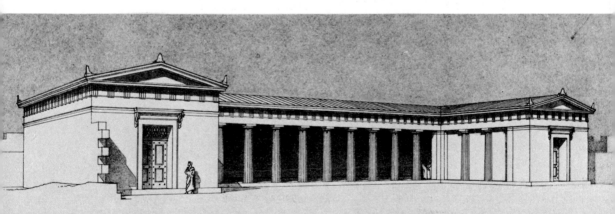

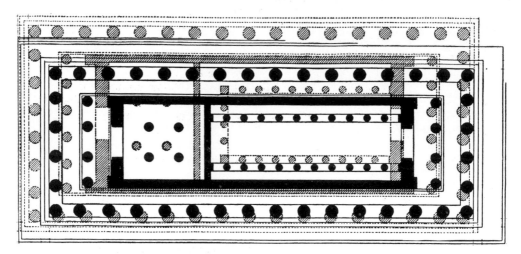

Plan of the three building phases of the Parthenon.The Iktinos Parthenon (III) is shown by the shaded columns, the older (II) with black columns, and the oldest (I) by its elongated Krepidoma, with doted lines.

and for the sculptured architectural members of the pediment was poros limestone, and the dimensions of its foundations must have been 32.71 by 16.24 meters.

The length of the Parthenon I corresponded to 100 attic feet, a fact which led to its identification with the temple referred to in literary sources and inscriptions as the "hekatompedos neos", or "Hekatompedon", a name which was later given to the Parthenon III. Originally, the theory that the "Hekatompedon" was located farther to the north was supported. This was the site of the "archaios neos" (ancient temple of Athena), in other words, the site of the foundations of the mycenaean palace, exactly to the south of the Erechtheion. Today, however, it seems more probable that this also was located at the same site as the existing Parthenon.

Very few pieces of the superstructure and sculptured embellishment of the temple are in existence today in the Museum on the Acropolis.

The Parthenon I, or "archaic Parthenon" whose building began before the era of the Athenian tyranny, seems to have been preserved for the duration of an entire century, since its substitution with the Parthenon II took place after the fall of the tyrants around 507 B.C., or a few years later, after the battle of Marathon in 490 B.C.

The Parthenon II

The Parthenon II, or "older Parthenon", which succeeded the archaic temple of Athena on the same site, was also doric in style, was constructed of marble, and had dimensions much larger than the former Parthenon. This temple was never completed. At the time of the Persian invasion in 480 B.C., the building of the temple had just begun. The temple, whose "krepidoma" (substructure with three steps) had already been built, along with the first three drums of all the columns, was set fire to, and destroyed by the Persians, following the fortune of all the other monuments on the sacred rock of the Acropolis.

The temple, with a "pronaos" (portico) to the east, a "cella", an "opisthodomos", (recessed porch in the rear of a greek temple, sometimes enclosed with bronze grilles and serving as a treasury) to the west, and a large chamber between the latter and the cella, was meant to be a hexastyle with sixteen columns, along the flanks. The inner

34

building was "tetrastyle-prostyle" at both ends, that is an "amphiprostylos naos" (with columns at both ends), having access to the large west chamber through the opisthodomos, which also had four tall columns in its interior for the purpose of supporting the roof. The cella had two superposed rows of interior columns, which divided it in three aisles along its length.

The remains of the poros -krepidoma of the Parthenon were used as foundations of the Parthenon III, and may still be seen clearly at the southeast corner of the temple. Unfinished drums, bearing the traces of fire, are immured in the exterior side of the northern wall of the Acropolis (Themistocles' wall) and are still visible, as well.

The Parthenon (Parthenon III)

Following the Persian invasion, an entire generation, the generation of the victors of 480 B.C., left its imprint in history before the Athenians thought of re-building a temple for the worship of Pallas Athena, the Virgin goddess, on the rock of the Acropolis.

The building of the Parthenon (Parthenon III) began in 447 B.C., at the exact site of the burned, destroyed, half-completed temple of the goddess, while its substructure was used for the foundation of the new temple.

The building of the Parthenon lasted ten years. In 438 B.C. (85th Olympiad) the temple was dedicated during the celebration of the Panathenaic festival. However, in order to complete the sculpture of the reliefs of the pediment and the metopes, work continued for five more years, until 432 B.C.

The new Parthenon, which was a building belonging to Pericles' broader plan of embellishing and transforming Athens, was designed by the architects, Ictinos and Callikrates, who were responsible for its erection. Pericles entrusted, however, the general supervision of this project to Phidias, his friend, co-worker, and advisor on artistic matters.

The Parthenon, which was the most respected and largest of the resplendent sacred buildings on the Acropolis, rises majestically at the highest point of the rock. With its enormous bulk, it was visible from all points of the plain around Athens and the surrounding hills, and was the principle crowning feature of the entire area.

In order to obtain a picture of the size of the temple, one must keep in mind that the volume of the roofed area of the Parthenon — from the "stylobate" to the "entablature" — was approximately 22,500 cubic meters, while its area at the stylobate was 2,145 square meters. For purposes of comparison, it should be noted that the area of the Parthenon II, calculated at the stylobate, as well, was 1,823 square meters, while that of the Parthenon I (the "Hekatompedon"), calculated at the basis of the krepidoma was a mere 531 square meters.

The Parthenon is a doric "peripteral" temple (one whose cella is surrounded by a peristyle), with 8 columns at the shorter sides and 17 columns along the two longer flanks. This ratio of 8 × 17 columns is an exception of the rule in temple-building because, at that time, the usual ratio of doric temples had been established at 6 × 13 columns.

The structural sections of the Parthenon as we go from its lowest to a higher point are three: the *krepidoma, pteron* (the wing or flank colonnade of a temple) and the *entablature*. The horizontal arrangement of the parts of the temple has four sections: the *pronaos* (porch in front of the naos), the *cella* (the enclosed chamber or sanctuary of the temple), the *Hekatompedon*, or "Parthenon", and the *opisthodomos*.

The foundations of the Parthenon are visible practically in their entirety, and consist of the old poros krepidoma of the Parthenon II, and of a later projection towards the north, which become necessary after the increase in the width of the new temple. The visible foundation, with its great height, does not shock the viewer today, because it constitutes the basic substructure of the marble krepidoma, is essentially and organically tied with it, and contributes decisively to the structural and aesthetic loftiness of the temple.

The entire temple, as well as the krepidoma, was built of pentelic marble. Its dimensions at the stylobate were 69.616× 26.19 meters, with a total height from the "euthynteria" (the special top course of a foundation used as a levelling course) to the stylobate of 1.65 meters, with three steps of 0.55 meters in height, each.

Commencing with the lowest step of the krepidoma, which is not geometrically straight neither along the length, nor along the ends of the temple, but has a curvature of 0.11 meters high at the center of the long flanks, and of 0.066 meters at the center of the short ends, the aesthetic grandeur of the Parthenon begins to establish and makes itself felt. The curvature of the first step repeats itself in the two upper successive steps of the krepidoma. The walls of the temple rest on this curved surface of the krepidoma, and the doric colonnade which surrounds it, with columns set at equal distances except at the corners, stands up at its full height and becomes a decorative item, as well as the guard of the temple. Each of the columns of the pteron consists of ten to twelve drums, has a height of 10.433 meters, a diameter of 1.904 meters at its lower point and of 1.481 meters at the top, and has 20 flutes. As these columns rest on all four sides on the stylobate, they receive its curvature and convey it proportionately and equally to the architraves, while these, in turn, convey it to the diazoma of triglyphs and metopes, and, finally, to the cornice. By using this subtle curvature, the architects, Ictinos and Callicrates, succeeded in obtaining the rectilinear effect that they were striving for and had anticipated. They obtained a positive optical illusion (a restitution of the real) and avoided a negative optical illusion (a falsification of the real), which the use of aesthetically "cold" horizontal lines would have created.

At this point note must be made of all the other refined architectural solutions that were given by the creators of the Parthenon, in order to obtain a positive aesthetic result.

These are: the "entasis" (the slight convex curve given to the doric column in order to avoid a concave appearance) of the columns, that is the gradual diminution of their diameter beginning half-way up the column, the inward inclination of the colonnade of the "pteron", the convocation of the columns towards the center of the temple, the increase of the thickness of the four corner columns, the shortening of the intercolumnial distance of the end columns, and the gradual decrease in size of the metopes, from the center towards the ends of the frieze.

These solutions are characteristic of the grandeur of a highly aesthetic intellect, and are, simultaneously, the masterpiece of its application in practice.

The third perpendicular division of the temple, the entablature, which was composed of the "architrave", the "diazoma" (triglyphs-metopes), and the "cornice", was, along with the pediments, the culminating point of the entire architectural structure and had the stamp of a sculptured piece of work done by Phidias, one of the most famous Athenian sculptors of his time.

Examining, at this point, the floor plan of the Parthenon, we come to the pronaos which offered access to the temple's cella. This portico was bounded by the cella's eastern wall, its two antae and the colonnade, with the 6 slender doric columns in

View of the Parthenon from the south side.

front. As far as we can tell from the marks on the columns, the portico of the Parthenon was enclosed by a grilled fence.

One enters the main temple, the cella, from the pronaos. The cella was 30 meters long, this length corresponding, approximately, to 100 ancient Attic feet, a fact which justifies its name, "Hekatompedon". The cult statue of the goddess Athena was placed in this chamber. Two superposed doric colonnades, with 10 columns each, divided the length of the cella into three aisles, while a third superposed colonnade, along the rear, with square piers at the end, connected the former two behind the base of the cult statue, forming a Π, whose two long antennae faced the east, and were stopped by two pilasters, which were attached to the wall.

It is possible that these superposed colonnades created a gallery or upper aisle, which ran round the three sides of the interior of the cella.

As has already been mentioned above, the chryselephantine statue of Athena, the admirable work of Phidias, had been housed at the far end of this chamber, which was surrounded on three sides by colonnades. Extant today one may see remnants of the pedestal foundation, with dimensions of 4.09× 8.04 meters, as well as a hole in its center for the great beam that was the pivot of the wooden nucleus of the statue.

The statue had been made of gold and ivory. The dress of the goddess was made of sheets of gold, while the naked members of the body were made of ivory. These

The first good view in antiquity of the Parthenon (by G. Stevens).

precious materials were sculptured to adapt to a wooden interior and constituted its coating.

The golden parts, which according to calculations, weighed a little over a ton, could be easily removed, and checked for the accuracy of their weight. This resplendent chryselephantine statue, which was approximately 13 meters tall including the base, is said to have been lost during the 5th century A.D., when it was transported by the christians to Constantinople. The appearance of the statue is known to us from mediocre marble copies of the Roman era (Athena of Varvakeion at the National Museum and Athena Lenormant) which were smaller in size than the original. Pausanias, who saw the statue still in situ, in the middle of the second century A.D., has rendered a characteristic description. "The statue itself is made of ivory and gold. On the middle of her helmet is placed a likeness of the Sphinx .. and on either side of the helmet are griffins in relief .. The statue of Athena is upright, with a tunic reaching to the feet, and on her breast the head of Medusa is worked in ivory. She holds a statue of Victory about four cubits high, and in the other hand a spear; at her feet lies a shield and near the spear is a serpent. This serpent would be Erichtonius. On the pedestal is the birth of Pandora in relief".

The third chamber of the Parthenon, an area of 19.19× 13.37 meters is located to the west of the cella and was separated from it by a transverse wall. This wall is no longer in existence, giving the viewer the impression that the interior of the temple was comprised of only one section. This third chamber was the "oikos" (home) of the Parthenos (Virgin), and was called "the Parthenon". In the course of time, it gave its name to the entire temple which earlier had been named the "neos"(νεώς). In the center of this section, four ionic columns, resting on square bases or slabs, supported the roof. The four bases are still in situ today.

The "oikos" of the Virgin, which is also known as the opisthodomos and had no access to the cella, housed valuable articles (furniture, vessels, arms), the archives (a copper plaque with the inventory of the precious materials that had been used in the construction of the chryselephantine statue of Athena), as well as, the treasury (the treasury of the Athenian Confederacy after 438 B.C., and the treasury of the city of Athens).

According to an ancient source, this sacred and inviolable area of the "Parthenos" was used as the lodgings of Demetrios Poliorketes who transformed it to a place of orgies.

The sole access to this chamber is located at the center of its western wall and led to the Parthenon's fourth section, the main opisthodomos, which was exactly like the pronaos in form, shape and size. Valuable objects and the treasury of the goddess were secured in this area, which was also enclosed by a grilled fence.

Much later, when the Parthenon had been transformed into a christian church, three entrances were opened in the transverse wall between the cella and the opisthodomos.

To this day, one may see — at the southwest corner of the opisthodomos — the lower part of a mosque, a remnant and sample of the transformation of the Parthenon to a turkish shrine.

Ceiling. Roof

The ceiling of the main cella of the Parthenon (the "Hekatompedon" - Parthenon) was made of wood. However, the ceilings of the aisles, which were formed by the cella and the colonnades of the pteron, as well as the ceilings of the pronaos and opisthodomos were made of marble coffers with paintings. The roof of the temple was covered with marble tiles, which ended in marble antefixes.

At the four points where the marble "simae" (the terracotta or marble gutter of a building; on gables and sometimes on the flanks) of the temple's long flanks ended, outlets for the rain water, in the form of lion' s heads, had been placed.

The shorter sides of the temple ended in two pediments, which were decorated with colossal open-work marble flowery "acroteria" (the figures or ornaments at the lower angles or apex of a pediment, generally supported on plinths) at their angles and their apex.

The Zophoros of the Parthenon

The "zophoros" (frieze) of the Parthenon, with a height of one meter and a total length of 160 meters, encircled the top part of the walls of the cella, and the facades over the architraves of the opisthodomos and pronaos. The subject of this representation in relief was the procession of the Panathenaia.

The sculptured zophoros was one continuous band and began at the southwest corner of the opisthodomos. Using this corner as a starting point, the procession on the frieze followed opposite directions as the central theme unfolded uniformly and in succession, and finally closed at the central section of the frieze, on the facade of the temple.

View of the Parthenon from the Propylaea. To the right, the aisle of the krepidoma, between the south wall of the cella and the south colonnade of the pteron.

The three sides of the zophoros (the west, south, and north sides) represented phases, scenes and instant events during the procession, while the fourth, the east side, represented its end, with the presence of the gods of Olympos, that is the basic goal of the entire procession, the offering of the sacred ''peplos'' (veil) of the goddess to the high priest by the ''Arrephoroi'' (the maidens in waiting on Athena).

The zophoros of the procession of the Panathenaia was composed of 360 human figures, in groups, or standing as isolated entities, and a great number of animals. There were gods, priests, archons, musicians, riders, virgins bearing water jugs, or baskets, old men carrying ''thalluses'' (young stems and shoots of plants), citizens and women, young men, even horses, oxen, and rams. All the figures acted and moved towards an easterly direction, where the majestic, stately procession was brought to an end.

The sculptured composition of the zophoros, using such an intense, live theme, was executed under the inspiration and the plan of Phidias, the work of the sculptor himself and of his apprentices. It is indisputable that Zeus, Hera and Iris of the eastern section of the frieze are the work of Phidias' hands. Being a masterpiece of unparalle-

The door of the pronaos of the Parthenon (by G.Niemann).

Reconstruction of the chryselephantine statue of Athena (by A.K. Orlandos).

led strength, sculptured perfection and aesthetic beauty, the frieze of the Parthenon became, for many centuries during antiquity, the symbol and image of the most respected, the most brilliant, and the most solemn event that the Athenians experienced every year or so, with the repetition of the City-festival in honor of their protectress goddess.

Of the zophoros itself, only the slabs of its western side and some of the southern are still in situ on the Parthenon, many members having been destroyed by Morozini, while others lie in the Museum on the Acropolis.

The greatest number of slabs of the frieze are in the British Museum, having been snatched up by Elgin. One slab from the eastern side is at the Louvre and part of another in Vienna.

In contrast to the sculptured members of the frieze, which could not be easily viewed because the 46 columns of the pteron made their direct viewing extremely difficult, the "metopes" (the sculptured panels between the triglyphs) of the Parthenon were quite visible because they had been placed in a commanding position high on the temple's entablature. The metopes, alternating with the triglyphs, were placed on all four sides of the entablature. Each metope held two human figures, or a group of man and animal. The representations on the metopes have all used themes taken from mythology, but the themes were so chosen as to symbolize and remind the people of the earlier and more recent victorious struggles of the Greeks against enemies that had threatened their land and their freedom.

The sculptured reliefs and decorations of the metopes of the north side of the

Parthenon had scenes of the Trojan war as a unifying theme, on the west, scenes from the battle of the Athenians and Amazons, on the south scenes from the battle of the Lapiths against the Centaurs, and finally, on the eastern side, scenes from the struggle of the gods of Olympos against the "Gigantes" (giants in the greek mythology).

The metopes were completed by 440 B.C. It is questionable, however, whether they bear the stamp of the sculptured work of Phidias himself.

In general, the metopes suffered a great deal of damage during the explosion caused by Morozini. Besides those which were completely destroyed at that time, the remaining have suffered serious surface-deterioration which make the discernment of their outline difficult, the latter being true of the western, and especially, more so, of the eastern side. The metopes of the southern flank are the best preserved. Of these, one is in situ, three in the Museum on the Acropolis, and the others in the British Museum.

Only 11 metopes are in their original position on the northern flank. The rest were destroyed during the explosion of Morozini.

The Pediments

The sculptured embellishments of the pediments required five years 437 - 432 B.C. for their completion, and were the last pieces of work done on the Parthenon.

Each of the compositions of the pediments — length of "tympanon" (the triangular

The notheast corner of the eastern pediment of the Parthenon.

wall enclosed by the raking cornice of the pediment and the horizontal cornice of the entablature beneath) 28.35 and height in the center 3.45 meters — was 28 meters long and the figures in the center stood approximately 3 meters tall.

Altogether, the figures of the two compositions were over fifty in number, of which very few exist today. All those which had been preserved until Morozini's time and were saved from harm during the explosion, were snatched up by Elgin and are now in the British Museum.

The themes for both compositions were taken from mythology, and are of a special local character and meaning, since both refer to Athena.

The birth of the goddess Athena was represented with godlike majesty at the eastern pediment, right over the formal entrance to the temple. The two main figures of the theme, confront each other and command the center of the composition. Zeus, to the left, seated on his throne, with his sceptre in his left hand and thunder in his right, faced, standing in front of him, a fully armed and joyous Athena who had just been born from her father's head, after the latter had been struck a blow by Hephaistos, who is pictured behind the goddess, naked, standing, still holding the axe which he had just used.

Seated behind Zeus and Athena, correspondingly, are the figures of Hera and

Reconstruction of the southeast of the Parthenon.

Poseidon who, surprised by the event, have turned their eyes towards and are ecstatically looking at the miracle.

This composition, with other god-like figures who are looking upon and participating in the unexpected and pleasant event, unfolds to the right and left of the main figures. The left corner of the eastern pediment ends with the portrayal of the quadriga of the Sun who rises from the Ocean and is headed towards the center, as though to open the composition, while to the right, it closes with the Moon, on a quadriga, who is departing in order to sink in the Ocean, leaving behind her the brilliance and light of creation.

The western pediment, over the entrance of the opisthodomos which led to the "oikos" of the Virgin, portrays the myth of the contest between Poseidon and Athena for the possession and protection of Attica.

Athena and Poseidon are the central figures of the pediment. The gods who are represented holding their symbols, are shown standing in an intensely lively position.

The naked, robust body of Poseidon, who is forcefully being jolted backwards, is characterized by a nervous uncertainty about the outcome of the contest, while the lively and majestic position of Athena demonstrates her certainty about her victory. The symbols of the gods — the olive -tree and the spring of sea water, gifts of their

Reconstruction of the eastern facade of the Parthenon (by A.K. Orlandos).

offering for the possession of Attica — are shown near the two gods, in their representation on the pediment.

The chariots, which had brought the two antagonists to the rock of the Acropolis for the judgment, were also placed to the right and left of the gods. Athena's chariot was driven by Nike and Poseidon's by Amphitrite (the god's wife), or by one of the Nereids (sea nymphs). The chariots were accompanied by Hermes, and Iris, the messengers of the gods.

The remainder of the composition shows the statues of heroes, and other figures flanking the two gods. These were the arbitrators of the contest, Cecrops (founder and first king of Attica), and Erechtheus, with members of their families, also watching the events taking place. Kephissos, and Ilissos, or, possibly, two other heroic figures of Attica, were represented at the two corners of the pediment.

Each composition on the two pediments has a strictly uniform theme. Both are characterized by a serene, majestic, dramatic effect which reaches its apex at the center, and step by step, becomes calmer towards the ends. These compositions on the pediments of the Parthenon constitute the highest rank in the evolution of sculptured pedimental syntheses.

The distribution of the figures represented, their position, and the accommodation of their size to the binding predetermined triangular space of the tympanon of the temple, are especially admirable in the pediments of the Parthenon.

In spite of the controversies and the variety of opinions which have been expressed concerning the artist-creator of these pediments, there can be no doubt that this extraordinary creation bears the stamp and conception of the intellect, and the execution by the hands of the great Phidias and his apprentices.

46

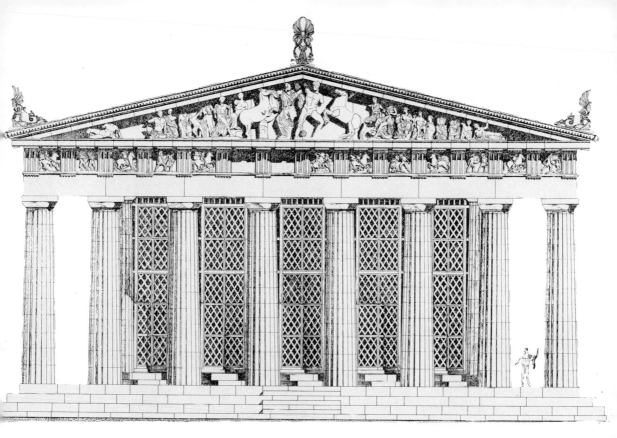

Reconstruction of the western facade of the Parthenon (by A.K. Orlandos).

The Temple of Roma and Augustus

The remains of a "monopteros" circular structure of the Ionic order, with a diameter of 8.60 meters at the exterior, may be seen to the east of the Parthenon (Plan, no **44**). From an inscription carved on a section of the architrave, we learn that the Athenians dedicated this building to the goddess Roma and Octavian Augustus, in order to appease the Emperor. This small temple, of white marble, which is surrounded by nine ionic columns,was certainly constructed after 27 B.C.,when Octavian became emperor. The height of the temple is calculated at 7.35 meters, at the cornice.

The Shrine of Pandion

The shrine of Pandion, the mythical king, son of Erechtheus and father of Aegeus, was located at a 25-meter distance to the east of the Parthenon, facing the southeast corner of the wall of the Acropolis (Plan, no **45**).

Today, only a section of the wall of the shrine is in situ, in the basement of the Museum of the Acropolis. Remains of walls, chiselling on the surface of the rock for the foundations of the walls, determine the form and shape of the shrine, which consisted basically of an enclosure separated into two open areas along its length, at a northwest-southeast axis.

The western area had a propylon at its northwest side, and the eastern area had a small entrance at the end of its south side. This shrine of Pandion, of the middle of the 5th century B.C., was obviously built after the construction of the Kimonian wall of the Acropolis. Due to filling-in with earth, and elevating this surface, it seems that an older shrine to Pandion disappeared under the rubble.

The NE corner of the Parthenon and the temple of Rome and Augustus (by G. Stevens).

The Shrine of Zeus Polieus

Close to the northeast corner of the Parthenon, at the highest level area of the surface of the rock, to the north of the temple of Roma, one came across the shrine of Zeus Polieus. Its location and shape are, basically, determined by chiselling on the rock which was used for the foundation of its walls (Plan, no **46**).

It seems that this shrine consisted of the sanctuary, which was located at the eastern end of the rock, and included a small temple "in antis", with an entrance to the north, a carved "bothros" (sacred pit) in its center for the remains of sacrifices, and a rectangular stone enclosure to the west, which had an entrance at its southwest corner, exactly opposite the corner of the Parthenon.

Pausanias refers to a strange and incomprehensible rite, which included the sacrifice of a bull, the "Diipoleia", and took place around an altar located at this spot, in honor of Zeus Polieus. He also refers to two statues, dedicated to Zeus, representing him in an archaic form, and a later piece of sculpture, done by Leochares (330 B.C.).

From Athenian coins, we know that Zeus Polieus was represented standing, with one hand elevated towards the back, holding a thunderbolt.

The shrine of "Gaia (earth) Karpophoros (fruitful)"

At a distance of only nine meters to the north of the seventh column of the Parthenon (counting from the norhwest corner of the colonnade), one comes upon the shrine of "Gaia Karpophoros (Plan, no **47**) according to the prophecy", as the inscription, which is carved on the rock at this point, states. It is certain that Pausanias saw "a statue of Gaia who is imploring Zeus to send some rain to the earth".....

The Altar of Athena

The primitive altar of Athena, who was co-worshipped with Erechtheus, was located to the east of the Erechtheion, and at a distance of 15 meters from the entrance of the "archaios neos" (Plan, no **48**).

The location of the altar at this spot is determined by chiselled marks on the rock. This was the main, the great altar of Athena on the Acropolis, and was used, through the centuries, by all the temples which were built, successively, at the site of the "archaios neos", that is, by the "Hekatompedon", and by the Erechtheion, later on, since the goddess Athena, while acquiring various identities, always remained basically the same.

The Ancient Temple of Athena

The foundations of an older temple of the 6th century B.C. (of the Peisistratids' era) are located to the south of the Erechtheion, and adjacent to it (Plan, no **49**). This temple was dedicated to Athena, and is the well-known temple of Athena Polias, or "archaios neos" (ancient temple). It was also located on the site of the mycenaean palace, of which we have essentially nothing extant today.

The area where the temple was situated had served, during the age of tyranny, as the site of three consecutive temples, was the most appropriate for building because it had already been leveled for the mycenaean palace, and, more important, because, as it seems, the palace itself was closely related to the worship of the goddess Athena and other gods and heroes.

It seems that the first of these three temples, the "πυκινὸς δόμος Ἐρεχθῆος" (well-constructed dwelling of Erechtheus), was built during the Geometric age. Essentially, we have no remains of this temple today, with the exception of two stone bases (in situ), enclosed by a low iron grille, and an "acroterion", made of bronze plate, depicting Gorgo among animals. These are the only remains which can be attributed to this temple, while, at one time, it was believed that the stone bases belonged to the mycenaean palace. The existence of this temple is believed to be certain. It is a point of controversy, however, whether this geometric temple was succeeded, in the 6th century B.C., by two different temples on the same site, or one with two building phases, during the same century, one sometime around 570 B.C., and the other in 525 B.C.

Reconstruction of the facade of the old temple of Athena (by W.Schuchhardt).

This problem continues to remain unsolved because it is difficult to discern the two temples, or to recognize two building-phases in one temple. Beginning with the 19th century A.D., the problem has strongly occupied the minds of Greek and foreign scholars, who puzzle both over the foundations of the temples and, especially, over the architectural members of its superstructure.

However, the foundations in view today (43.44× 21.43 meters) must be attributed to the poros-limestone and marble temple of 525 B.C., that is, the third temple which was "peripteral" (the cella of which is surrounded by a peristyle) doric, with a columnial ratio of 6× 12, a "pronaos", and an "opisthodomos" and "cella". The pronaos and opisthodomos had a "prostasis" (the exterior part of the temple between two antae) of four columns each, or two columns each, between the antae. The cella was divided by a transverse wall into two chambers, the eastern and the western one. The eastern chamber, which was practically a square, with two interior colonnades of 3 columns each, along its length, was divided into three aisles. This chamber housed the "ouranopetes xoanon" (heaven-sent xoanon) of the goddess Athena.

The western section was divided into three chambers. One entered an oblong section through the entrance of the opisthodomos from which two other entrances, on the eastern side, led to two separate rooms. It would seem that this tripartite division of the western section of the cella corresponds to the arrangement that was given later on to the Erechtheion, and represented the worship of an equivalent number of gods and heroes (Poseidon-Erechtheus, Hephaistos, Boutos).

The temple, and along with it, the offerings and the "ouranopetes xoanon" of the goddess were consumed by the fire set by the Persians in 480 B.C. Many fragments were immured in the northern wall of the Acropolis (Themistocles' wall).

It seems that, immediately after the end of the Persian Wars (479 B.C.), the Athenians restored parts of the temple's cella, which had obviously been saved from the destruction, and replaced the burnt "xoanon" with a new one, which was placed in the same spot as the old one. In this new form, that is, with a section of the cella only, and without exterior colonnades, the temple was used until 406 B.C., when the building of the Erechtheion was brought to completion.

This temple must have been the one referred to by ancient sources as the cella, the temple (neos), te ancient temple (archaios neos), the temple in the city, in which the ancient statue is housed, the temple of Athena, the temple, the shrine.

According to Xenophon, the temple was intentionally set fire to at the end of the 5th century B.C., in order to free the area and eliminate any obstruction to the view of the new temple, the Erechtheion, where the "xoanon" of the goddess had been transported in the meantime.

The remains of the temple that may be seen today, as well as, the architectural members of the superstructure, and pieces of its sculptured decorations, which are to be found in the Museum on the Acropolis, had been attributed, by scholars in the past, to the "Hekatompedon" temple of Athena Parthenos (the Parthenon I).

The Erechtheion

Commanding the northern side of the rock of the Acropolis, the Erechtheion is an unmatched work of art, and a harmonious complement of the area across from the Parthenon.

The Erechtheion (Plan, no **50**), one of the most highly decorated and original creations of ancient greek architecture, was constructed in order to replace the "ancient temple" (archaios neos) of Athena and, along with the temple of Nike, represents the "rich style" on the sacred rock. The ancient myths concerning the founding of the city were connected with this temple and the traditional types of worship were transferred there from the "archaios neos".

The construction of the Erechtheion started during the Peace of Nikias (421 - 415 B.C.), but it seems that it was interrupted after the resumption of hostilities between Athens and Sparta (Sicilian Campaign), and then was completed around 406 B.C. An inscription which was found on the Acropolis, and referred to its construction, is dated 409 - 408 B.C., and mentions that an architect named Philocles supervised the work on the Erechtheion.

The Erechtheion, which owes its name to Erechtheus, was dedicated to the worship of Athena and deified Erechtheus, who was a local hero and mythical king of Athens. Erechtheus is identified with Erichthonios, the son of Hephaistos and Gaia, who was brought up by Athena, while later on, during the Classical era, he was identified with Poseidon. We assume, therefore, that the Erechtheion, a double temple, was dedicated to Athena and Poseidon (co-temple gods) who are also associated with this specific locale of the sacred rock by their contest over the possession of the soil of Attica. According to Pausanias, Hephaistos, the father of Erichthonios, and the hero Boutes, brother of Erechtheus, were also worshipped in this temple.

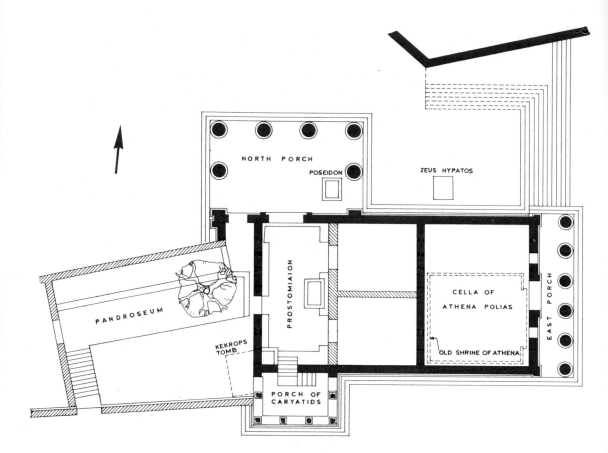

NORTH PORCH

POSEIDON

ZEUS HYPATOS

PROSTOMIAION

PANDROSEUM

KEKROPS
TOMB

CELLA OF
ATHENA POLIAS

EAST PORCH

OLD SHRINE OF ATHENA

PORCH OF
CARYATIDS

Restored plan of the Erechtheion

The Erechtheion presents a unique picture, both in its exterior form, as well as, in the interior arrangement of the various chambers and levels of the cella. The temple, with dimensions of 22.22 × 11.62 meters in the cella, on its eastern side appears to be a normal prostyle ionic temple with six columns of a 6.59 meter height. The northern column of this side may be seen in the British Museum along with the other Elginian marble pieces. The floor of the western side of the temple is approximately 3 meters lower than that of the eastern side. On the lower section of the western wall there is another wall — between the antae of the cella — upon which rest the four supports of the entablature, of á 5.62 meter height. These four supporting members have the appearance of semi-detached columns on the exterior and of antae in the interior. Aside from the opening between one semi - detached column and the southern anta, a low parapet, with a grille over it closed all the other openings between the semi-detached columns. Two unusual "prostases", or porticoes may be seen along the long flanks of the temple. The northern portico, with dimensions of 5.40 × 8.17 meters, is also called "the Prostasis towards the doorway", is at a lower level than the southern portico, and provides a shelter for the entrance which leads to the western part of the temple. This portico is composed of a krepidoma with 3 steps, of 6 ionic columns (4 × 2), of a 7.635 meter height, have a small inward incline, "an entasis", and a "meiosis" (a slightly smaller diameter at the upper part of the column), juts out of the western boundary of the temple by 3 meters, creating a second row or piers along the lengthened part of the northern wall of the cella. On the pavement to the left of the entrance, at the spot where the part of the roof has been removed an altar of "Zeus Supreme", or of "Thyechoos" who is known from inscriptions to have belonged to the Athenian priesthood, was to be found. Pausanias reports that, instead of sacrifices, "pemmata" (sweet bread) were offered at this altar. The grave of Erechtheus was to be found at the location of this portico.

The portico of the Korae (Karyatids) is to be found at the south side of the temple, and corresponds with the northern portico. This latter portico is much smaller in size than the northern one, has a three-stepped krepidoma, which is a continuation of that of the eastern and southern flanks of the temple. This portico is composed of a parapet, of a 1.77 meter height, which supports the 6 Korae (4 × 2), who, in turn, support the entablature and the roof. There is a small entrance at the eastern short side of the parapet. Through a secret passage, the entrance led to a staircase, the grave and shrine of Cecrops (Cecropion), which was quite low, under the southwest side of the Erechtheion.

It is extremely difficult today to discern the original plan of the interior of this temple because the Erechtheion is one of the monuments of the Acropolis which has undergone radical changes, during the years following antiquity. During the early medieval times, the Erechtheion became a christian basilica, during the Frankish domination it was the palace of the latin prince of the area, while, during the Turkish occupation it served as the home of the Commander of the Turkish garrison. At this time, the floor was dug deep for the construction of cisterns, one at the western section of the cella, at the location of the "Erechtheis Sea", and another at the eastern. In spite of these radical changes, re-arrangements, and additions, which resulted in the alteration of the interior of the temple, according to evidence and traces that have been preserved up to our time, scholars have reached the conclusion that the temple had been divided by a transverse wall, into two chambers, an eastern and a western one.

The eastern section of the cella with a length of 7.318 meters, had two windows — 2.70 × 0.75 meters — on its eastern side, to the right and left of the entrance (2.70 meters wide), opposite the ionic portico. This chamber of the cella had been dedicated to the worship of "Athena Polias", patron goddess of the city, and housed the cult statue of the goddess (the sacred wooden statue, the statue of a sitting god, the idol, or xoanon of the springs, that which was made of olive wood) to which the "Arrephoroi" offered the veil of the Panathenaia, which was woven in gold. The famous golden lamp, which had been made by the sculptor Callimachos, burned its inextinguishable light in front of the "xoanon". An exceedingly tall bronze palm-tree reached the wooden roof and was used to draw out the smoke, as Pausanias reports.

The western chamber of the cella which was three meters lower than the eastern, had a tripartite division, which would seem to be comparable to the division of the corresponding chamber of the "archaios neos". On its eastern side, this western section had two smaller apartments, with entrances which led to an anteroom that is, the "prostomiaion" (the first rectangular section after the northern stoa of the Erechtheion, also called a "prostasis"), whose entrance was the gate of the northern portico. The anteroom communicated with the portico of the Korae through a small opening on its southern side. Along with the altar of Poseidon, one found altars of Boutes and Hephaistos in this chamber, which was dedicated to the worship of Poseidon-Erechtheus. The "oikouros ophis" (guardian home snake), symbol of the "chthonian" (underworld) cult lived in this chamber. Originally, this snake was Erechtheus, or Erichthonios. Athena had an immediate connection with the snake, Erichthonios, and

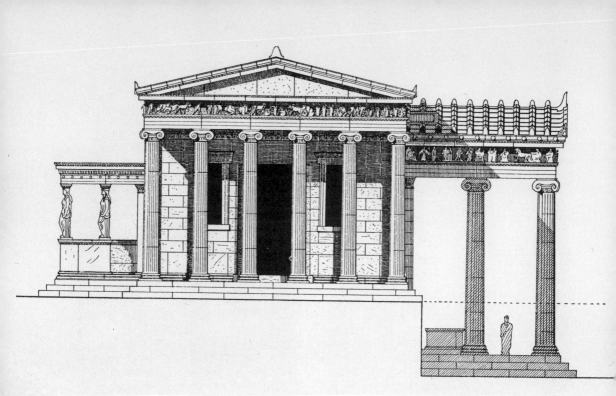

East elevation (above), and west elevation (down) of the Erechtheion (by G. Stevens).

this was the reason why snake was represented on the chryselephantine statue of the goddess in the Parthenon.

According to legend, during the contest between Poseidon and Athena, the former struck the rock at this spot and sea-water (the Erechtheis Sea) gushed out. Pausanias calls this the "well", and it was located under the pavement of the anteroom. The opening of the well ("prostomiaion") seems to have been the reason for the name of this area. The names of the priests of the Eteouboutadae lineage, who were the hereditary priests of the co-temple gods, Poseidon-Erechtheus and Athena Polias, were inscribed on the wall of the western chamber. Contrary to an older belief concerning these chambers, where the co-temple gods were worshipped in the Erechtheion, the Greek scholar John Travlos has recently formulated the opinion that Poseidon-Erechtheus was worshipped in the eastern chamber and Athena Polias in the western one. The open area between the northern wall of the cella and the eastern side of the northern portico had been paved and was used as a court. The marble staircase which led to the higher level and facilitated the communication with the eastern section of the temple began at the eastern boundary of the court.

Pedimental roofs had been erected over the entablature, the cella and the northern portico. The roof of the northern portico was at a lower level and its axis was perdendicular to the roof of the cella. The portico of the Korae, with its own entablature, had a level roof.

Due to the separately attached architectural structures (northern portico and Korae portico), the Erechtheion does not have the expected and accepted form of the simple rectangular shape, which the ancient greek temples had on the whole. The disruption of the unity of the building is intensified by the difference in the height between the krepidomata and the roofs.

The uniformity and harmonious relationship of the entablature, the cella, and the northern portico, as well as, the continuous, uniform krepidoma of the eastern and southern side of the temple, restore the cohesion of the building.

The general plan and the architectural oddities that one observes on the exterior form and the interior plan of the various chambers of the Erechtheion are caused by a truly wise conception of the architect:

a) to cope with the topography of the area, upon which the new temple was to be built. The topography of the rock had steep slopes and great variations in the altitudes of the various levels, which he did not level by filling it up because he wanted to preserve the sacred "martyria" (proofs, tokens).

b) to face up to the need for the preservation and collection — under the same roof — of the ancient sacred signs, which could be seen in this location (the traces of the trident and the Erechtheis Sea, the sacred olive tree, the nest of the guardian home snake, the graves of Cecrops and Erechtheus).

c) to seek solutions to the demands and needs imposed by the worship and religious practices, which were transferred from the "archaios neos" and, then, practiced in the new building.

The Erechtheion which, on the whole, is a rich, light, graceful, refreshing building, with sensitivity and refinement, is especially cared for in its architectural details, and sculptured embellishments.

The Attic grace of the Ionic order is pictured in the columns, whose slenderness is especially accented in those of the eastern portico, with sculptured compound ribs on

Southwest corner of the Erechtheion.

the upper spirals of the bases, which are repeated on the capitals, above the "echinos" (the convex moulding of circular plan with egg-and-dart placed under the cushion of the ionic capital), with sculptured "anthemia" (a continuous pattern of alternating palmette and lotus, often rising from nests of acanthos leaves and connected scrolls) of the "hypotrachelium" or neck with the ionic "cymation" (a wave moulding of double curvature), which decorated the echinos and was repeated on the "abacus" (the upper-most member of a capital, moulded in the Ionic order and curved out over the canted white of the special ionic capital used at the corner of a building), and, finally, with the double spiral ribs of the capitals, which were countersunk between the convolutions, in each case with a gilt bronze stem ending in a group of rosettes in the eyes of the volutes.

The "anthemia" which decorate the architrave of the antae of the cella of the northern portico, and form one continuous belt on the upper part of the long flanks, exactly below the architrave, lend exceptional beauty to the temple.

However, that which on the exterior renders exceptional brilliance to the entire temple, was the "zophoros" (frieze of a 0.62 meter height) of the cella and the northern portico. The figures of the zophoros, sculptured in white pendelic marble, had been attached on slabs of dark blue Eleusinian marble.

The theme, or subject of the representations on the zophoros has not been made clear, in spite of the fact that quite a few pieces have been preserved, and are now housed in the Museum on the Acropolis. It is quite possible that the central theme was

The Karyatids of the South portico of the Erechtheion.

related to mythical Attic figures (Ion, Cecrops, Erechtheus, Eumolpos, etc.). The name of the artist who designed the representations is also unknown. From an extant inscription, we do know, however, the names of some of the artisans who carved the figures.

The figures of the zophoros of the northern portico are a little larger than the figures of the zophoros of the cella. All these figures are characterized by refined workmanship, grace, liveliness and a true-to-nature appearance.

All three pediments of the Erechtheion (two in the cella, and one at the northern portico) did not have pedimental sculptures. The corners of the pediments carried marble decorative vases ("acroteria") and the "cyma" (a wave moulding of double curvature), which was crowned by flower-shaped rampart antefixes, was surmounted by lions' heads.

The form, and workmanship around the great doorway of the northern portico holds a special position among the entire sculptured decoration of the Erechtheion.

This gate, certainly the most official one, was magnificent and luxurious, and constituted the most beautiful prototype of an entrance to an ancient temple. In antiquity, sometime toward the end of the first century B.C., it was restored and so presents variations in the quality of the workmanship, which is most apparent in the palmettes and rosettes of the door lintel which were replaced during the reparation. The polychrome coffers of the roof complement the decoration of the portico.

57

*Portico of the Karyatids
(by G. Stevens).*

The apex, however, of the artistic expression of the Erechtheion is to be found at the southern portico of the temple, with the presence of the Korae (Karyatids) who dominate the entire area with their beauty and majestic appearance. The six Korae, which have been placed in a Π-shaped formation, marvellously support the ceiling of the southern portico of the Erechtheion, according to an old custom of Greek architecture.

The Korae of the Erechtheion are lithe, light, and full of spirit and youth, three of them gracefully bending the left, and the other three the right leg, in such a manner that — on the outside — one sees only the perpendicular folds of their garments, similar to the flutings of columns, thus breaking the ceremonial, static rigidity of their posture.

When viewing the Karyatids one has a feeling that they are marching in a religious procession, carrying a basket full of offerings, on their heads, whole-heartedly dedicated to a sacred duty on the grave of Cecrops, an eternal symbol of aesthetic perfection and an indestructible assertion of human values.

The Precinct of Pandrosos

The precinct of Pandrosos, or Pandroseion, is located across the two-storied western side of the Erechtheion, a shrine dedicated to the cult of Pandrosos, one of the daughters of Cecrops (Plan, no **51**).

The Pandroseion, with a low enclosure, included the small temple of the daughter of Cecrops, and the sacred olive-tree of Athena, under which an altar of Herkeios Zeus was located, and was preserved from the period of the mycenaean palace to the 4th century B.C., at least.

The Arrephorion

The building of the "Arrephoroi", about which Pausanias states that it was not far from the temple of Athena Polias, the Erechtheion, has been identified with the foundations of the structure, which are located at the limits of the northern wall of the Acropolis, across from, and a little to the west of the precinct of Pandrosos (Plan, no **52**).

The Arrephorion consists of a long, narrow chamber (8.50× 4.50), with an entrance at the center of its long southern side, which faced a stoa with four columns at its facade.

The Arrephorion communicated with the cavern of Pan and the Aglaureion — the shrine of another daughter of Cecrops which was located exactly under the building — through secret passages, and staircases under the fortification wall.

The Arrephoroi, who were young girls, 7 - 11 years old, and had been chosen from the well-known families of Athens, performed secret rites by transporting the covered "unspoken of sacred objects" which they, themselves, were not allowed to look upon. Then, having descended the secret staircase and passed by the Aglaureion, they handed them to the priest of the neighboring shrine of Aphrodite. Once there, they were offered, by the priests, other similar covered sacred objects which, in turn, they conveyed to the priestess of Athena, having returned by the same route.

This secret ceremony of the Arrephoroi, and the objects which the girls conveyed — snake-like and phallus-shaped cookies, "likenesses to dragons and men's shapes", possibly even the branches of pine-trees (thalluses) — symbolized the growth of fertility and the sowing of the fields.

Athena Promachos

After their victory and defeat of the Persians at the battle of the river Eurumedon, and, especially, after they had collected money from the sale of the persian spoils, the Athenians dedicated a colossal statue — a "bronze statue of Athena, from the Medes who had disembarked at Marathon, done with the art of Phidias and offered as a prize" — which was offered with honors to Athena Promachos who had helped them in their struggle against the barbarians.

The imposing statue of the goddess, which must have been one of Phidias' earlier pieces, was placed at a most efficacious spot, approximately 37 meters in the exact front of the entrance to the Propylaea, to the west of the processional way (Plan, no **53**). With its larger-than life, tremendous size (7 meters tall standing alone and 9 meters tall with its marble pedestal) it commanded the sacred rock, and had been visible to the voyagers at sea, those who arrived from Cape Sounion.

The statue of Athena Promachos, and votive offerings located between the Erechtheion and the Parthenon (by G. Stevens).

Standing tall, on her pedestal, this bronze Athena wore a doric veil (peplos), and supported a spear in her raised right arm, a spear which, with its point up, stood taller than her helmet, holding, a shield, with the left hand, which rested perpendicularly next to her.

The shield depicted in relief a representation of the Centauromachy. This representation was the design of the painter Parrasios, while the metal of the shield had been engraved by Mys, the engraver.

Athena Promachos was one of the most famous statues of the ancient world and the largest in size on the Acropolis. As an ancient source reports "she supervised the festival", following the Panathenaic procession from its beginning, at the Dipylon, to its arrival on the Acropolis.

Athena Promachos, a respected jewel on the Acropolis, symbolized the faith that the people of Athens had in Peace, and, simultaneously, proclaimed their determined, undefeated, victorious strength in defensive, patriotic warfare.

What we have today, at the site where it stood, are traces of the statue's pedestal, with dimensions of 5 × 5 meters, marks of chiselling of its borders on the rock, and a few stone-plinths.

The Votive Offerings

As the case was with all the large greek shrines, so it was on the Acropolis of Athens, as well, the most important, the richest shrine of all. It was natural to offer and raise the "beautiful" offerings of the devoted pilgrims, "agalmata" for the goddess, gifts which

60

would please her and help create a pleasant disposition on her part. Practically totally lost, hundreds of votive offerings were placed on the sacred rock, inside the temples and in the open air, inside and outside the sanctuaries of small and large temples and shrines, on the krepidomata; all of them offerings that were made during the many centuries of ancient greek life on the Acropolis.

Chiselling marks on the rock which supported their pedestals, pieces of the statues themselves and of their bases, dedicatory inscriptions which have survived, literary evidence and, especially, Pausanias' descriptions speak of the existence of all these votive offerings on the Acropolis.

The age of the Peisistratids is especially rich in offerings, and the entire free space on the Acropolis was filled with votive offerings of faith and piety, offers to the beloved goddess of the Athenians. The persian destruction, which was a catastrophe for the monuments of the sacred rock, was the cause of the salvation of a large number of the votive offerings of this period, especially. By piously "burying" (in an area adjacent to the Parthenon) the dismembered offerings when these were excavated by the Archaeological Society at the end of the 19th century, they were restored to us.

However, the numerous votive offerings, which were placed on the Acropolis after the Persian Wars, up until the end of the ancient worship, have all but disappeared completely. Pausanias describes and offers information about the most important ones, which were still extant during his time, and which he was able to see.

THE ACROPOLIS MUSEUM

The Acropolis Museum belongs to that category of Museums, whose contents are indissolubly connected to one particular archaeological site, housing, as it does, the remains of the shrine, those that were not uprooted from the site, and express the majesty of conception and workmanship of the unparalleled masterpieces to be found on the sacred rock; those great, unique, inspirations of the human mind.

John Miliades bend over and embrassed the entire treasure with love, inspiration, wisdom, a spirit of inquiry, and caution as to how he could render these masterpieces — the marks of a cult already thousands of years old — accessible to man, as to how each person could make them part of his own being.

Having already visited the Acropolis, upon entering the Museum one sees the Acropolis, tries to bridge the centuries, and attempts, with his imagination, to place each piece in its proper location, or, if he so fancies, on the site one would prefer to see it standing.

In this guide, we refer and present a carefully chosen selection of certain outstanding characteristic masterpieces.

The Museum has nine Rooms, each with a personality of its own. Before entering the Museum proper, one may see in the courtyard cornices of Pentelic marble, which are derived from the northern portico of the Erechtheion, the bodies of horses, and a marble base with representations of athletes. A variety of finds may be found in the Lobby, having been assembled from different locations on the Acropolis. These are sculptured pieces, architectural members, bases from votive offerings, one Hermaic stele, and a marble lecythos (funerary marble vase).

There is a unity among the pieces which are exhibited in Room I. They are mainly poros limestone, and marble sculptures from pedimental compositions which, for the most part, decorated the small temples (treasuries) of the Archaic period, such as the Parthenon I.

Room II, which also contains sculptured pieces from the embellishment and decoration of the Archaic period, also houses votive offerings of the same period, male and female statues, statues of sphinxes, and representations of animals. A variety of ceramic statuettes and tiles, of the 6th century B.C., all of them humble offerings to the goddess, may be seen in the show-cases.

In Room III the presentation of pieces, from the sculptured decorations of 6th century temples, is continued, along with their architectural members, as well as, representations in relief, and statues of the "Kore" type, and of female figures in a sitting position.

Aside from the great variety of masterpieces of sculptured pieces, Room IV is characterized by the presentation of a majestic series of "Korae", which instill a special spirited quality with their liveliness and grace.

Dominant, in Room V, we find the magnificent pediment of the Gigantomachy of the "archaios neos" of Athena, which was restored and renovated by the Peisistratids around 525 B.C., as well as, a statue of outstanding beauty, the "Antenor Kore".

All the pieces from older excavations on the sacred rock (all the marble pieces), and from more recent ones, which were carried on at the south side of the Acropolis after the Second World War, had been placed by John Miliades in show-cases in the Alcove, adjoining Room V.

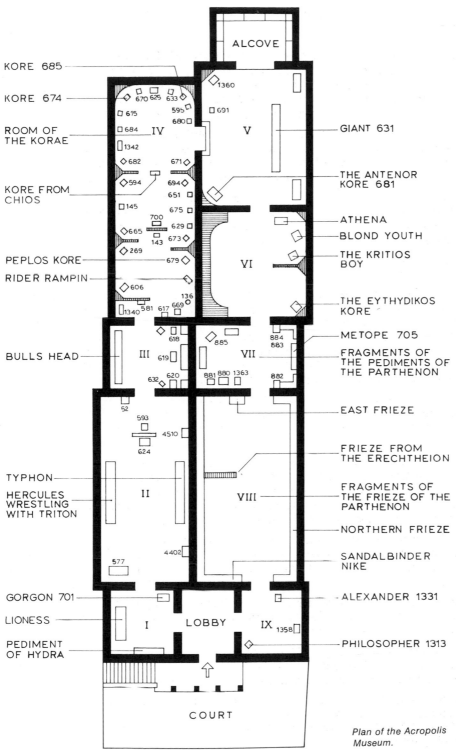

ALCOVE

KORE 685
KORE 674
ROOM OF
THE KORAE
KORE FROM
CHIOS
PEPLOS KORE
RIDER RAMPIN

1360
691
670 625 633
595
680
615
684 IV V
1342
682 671
594 694
651
145 675
700 629
665 143 673
269 679
606 136
1340 581 617 669
618 885
619 III VII
632 620 881 880 1363
52 884 883
593 882
4510
624

GIANT 631
THE ANTENOR
KORE 681
ATHENA
BLOND YOUTH
THE KRITIOS
BOY
THE EYTHYDIKOS
KORE
METOPE 705
FRAGMENTS OF
THE PEDIMENTS OF
THE PARTHENON
EAST FRIEZE

VI

FRIEZE FROM
THE ERECHTHEION

TYPHON
HERCULES
WRESTLING
WITH TRITON

II VIII

FRAGMENTS OF
THE FRIEZE OF THE
PARTHENON
NORTHERN FRIEZE
SANDALBINDER
NIKE

577
4402

GORGON 701
LIONESS
PEDIMENT
OF HYDRA

I LOBBY IX 1358

ALEXANDER 1331

PHILOSOPHER 1313

COURT

*Plan of the Acropolis
Museum.*

63

In Room VI, the exhibits, the male and female marble statues, as well as, the reliefs which were all votive offerings to the temples and shrines of the Acropolis, represent the most perfect, and powerful sculptured work that the Late-archaic period, and the period of the "Severe Style" had to offer the sacred rock.

Rooms VII and VIII have an unmatched and tragic unity. They include the remains of the sculptured decoration of the Parthenon, the Erechtheion, and the temple of Athena Nike, which were saved from destruction and pillage, and were buried and forgotten in the sacred soil of the rock.

Finally, Room IX, also known as the "Room of Procne", after the famous statue of this mythical figure, is a piece executed by the sculptor Alcamenes. This Room houses a variety of other objects, especially statues of different periods and categories.

The head of Alexander, as well as that of a philosopher, possibly the neoplatonic philosopher Plutarch, are among the most outstanding sculptured pieces in this room.

Lobby

1338. *Base of Atarbos:* A marble inscribed base of a bronze votive offering. The base is decorated with the representation of a dance worked in relief, and belongs to the 4th century B.C.

To the left, the choragos is depicted wearing a chiton (tunic) and himation, while at his right, two groups, of four naked dancers each, walk in rhythm holding shields in their left hand. This representation is characterized by harmony, gracefulness, and a musical quality in the movement of the figures.

1347. *Owl:* A marble owl of the beginning of the 5th century B.C. It is a severe symbol of Athena's wisdom, and was carved out of cycladic marble.

Room I

1. *The pediment of the Hydra:* A poros limestone pediment (length 6 meters) from a small unknown building of the beginning of the 6th century B.C. Hercules' labour — his effort to overcome the Lernaia Hydra — is depicted in low relief. The Hydra is aided in her confrontation by a crab. Hercules is wielding his club, while Iolaos, who is behind Hercules, is watching the contest, standing on a chariot.

4. *Lioness devouring a calf:* A poros limestone group of a lioness, who is tearing a calf to pieces. It is part of the right side of an archaic pediment of the beginning of the 6th century B.C. It is possible that the group belonged to the western pediment of the Parthenon I (Hekatompedon).

701. *Head of a Gorgon:* The marble archaic head of a Gorgon (beginning of the 6th century B.C.), most probably, was part of the central acroterion of the Parthenon I (Hekatompedon).

The monstrous character of the figure has been depicted by the archaic attic sculptor with characteristic clarity and liveliness of form.

1. The pediment of the Hydra.
1338. Base of Atarbos.

1347

701

1347. Owl
701. Head of a Gorgon.
630. Sphinx.
4. Lioness devouring a calf.
35. The tricorpor demon.

630

Room II

630. *Sphinx:* A marble archaic votive sphinx (560 - 550 B.C.), which had been placed on a tall column. Contrary to custom, the expression of her face, which is facing front (instead of sideways as was customary), shows intelligence, self-confidence, characteristic features of her supernatural nature. The expression of her face, which is created by her wonderful smile, gives an unbelievable quality of perfection and indescribable grace to this piece of sculpture.

35. *The tricorpor demon:* A poros limestone archaic pedimental composition of the beginning of the 6th century B.C. It belonged to a large temple, probably to the Parthenon II, of the "archaios neos" of Athena. The central figures of the pediment have been lost. Hercules is wrestling with Triton — a sea-monster — on the left side. A tricorpor demon, that is, the three male figures, merging into twisting snake-like tails, is depicted on the right side. Each of the male figures holds, in his human hand, one of the symbols of the elements of nature — a bird (the air), water, and fire.

With characteristic attic workmanship, the artist has attributed human vigour and strength to the Hercules group, and to the tricorpor demon a glorious smile, a simplicity of form, an expressive nobility and a rich, human quality of its soul.

624. *Moschophoros (Calf bearer):* A marble attic archaic group, of approximately 570 B.C., represents a strong, well-built, handsome man, (R)ombos, or (K)ombos, carrying a calf on his shoulders, his offering to Athena. He is dressed in a tight-fitting tunic, with the front of his body completely uncovered and his arms naked below the elbows.

The perfect quality, the beauty of the group, may be seen on the chest of the figure, the crossing of the male arms, the legs of the animal, which are interwoven symmetrically and frame the beautiful, pure, truthful male head, accompanied, on the right, by the innocent, trusting head of the animal bending confidently towards its master's head, while it follows him in its pre-destined fate of sacrifice to the goddess.

577. *Horses from a quadriga:* Four marble bodies of horses, parts of a votive quadriga, an attic archaic piece of work of approximately 570 B.C. A symmetrical harmony and an aesthetic simplicity characterize the composition in its entirety and its details.

Room III

3. *Bull's head (detail):* A poros limestone pedimental composition, depicting two lions attacking a bull. It is possible that this composition belonged to the "archaios neos" of Athena, or the Parthenon I (570 - 560 B.C.). To the right and left of the group, pieces of the lions' legs may be seen, along with the collapsed body of the bull.
The dramatic expression of the vanquished, dying animal, which is filled with pain, has been depicted with exceptional realism.

632. *Sphinx:* A marble attic archaic votive sphinx of the second half of the 6th c.B.C. (540 - 530 B.C.). The sphinx, which used to stand on a tall stele, faces frontwards, while its body is turned sideways. Its youthful face looks on with gentleness, goodness, and sweetness; features which manage to remove the demonic quality of the figure.

632

577

577. Horses from a quadriga.
632. Sphinx.

590. *The rider Rampin.*
624. *Moschophoros (Calf bearer).*

Room IV

590. *The rider Rampin* *: A marble statue of a rider, the most ancient piece extant, is one of the most significant Attic sculptured pieces of the 6th century B.C. (middle). Its unknown great creator must have worked on the statue sometime during 560 - 540 B.C. Extant today, we may see the upper part of the body and a piece of the horse's head with remains of its mane. The head is a plaster copy of the original, which may be found in the Louvre Museum, while a few pieces of the same workmanship, which have been placed next to the statue of the rider, prove that there must have been yet one more equestrian statue. The rider sits on his horse naked, has turned his head towards the left, in contrast to the head of his horse,which is turned towards the right. Its outlines and the anatomical details of its body, and especially of its face, declare the existence of a great sculptor, while the noble bearing and distinguished, polite expression, reveal the majesty with which he wanted to endow the sculptured rider, who belonged to an outstanding, distinguished family. It is possible that this rider, along with the one next to him, were a group, which represented the sons of Peisistratos, Hippias and Hipparchos.

*The name Rampin, has been given to the statue because the head of the rider belonged, originally, to the private collection of Rampin.

679. *Peplos Kore:* A marble archaic statue of a Kore, dedicated to Athena, a piece of approximately 530 B.C., probably the work of the same artist, who worked on the group of the rider Rampin.
   The Kore with the decorated youthful head, stands unbending and straight, dressed in a simple, unpleated, multi-colored doric veil, and a long chiton, is full of girlish liveliness and vigour, and, literally, sparkles with youthful beauty.

143. *Hunting dog:* A marble hunting dog, the outstanding work of an attic sculptor of the end of the 6th century B.C. (sometime in 520 B.C.), may, probably, be a piece of the same artist,who worked on the pediment of the Gigantomachy (number 631), or the group of the rider Rampin. The position and movement of the dog, who is extant in its entirety, and the pieces of another one, similar to it, which were found close to it, have led to the hypothesis that those two dogs were the guards at the entrance of the shrine of Brauronia Artemis.

702. *Hermes and the Graces:* A votive offering relief with a representation of Hermes, playing the double flute, followed by three female figures, holding hands, and moving in a rhythm suggesting a dance. Various interpretations have been given, concerning the three female figures of this representation (Graces, Nymphs, Aglaurides, or simply mortal women who are celebrating). The smaller figure behind them, and to the right, is believed to be Erichthonios as a child, or the offerer of the statue. This is a piece of simple artistic workmanship of the last decade of the 6th century B.C.

675. *Kore (from Chios):* This statue of a Kore, of the end of the 6th century B.C., is one of the most beautiful creations of the archaic ionic sculptured art, is probably, the work of an unknown Chian artist, as its characteristic workmanship indicates.

679. *Peplos Kore.*

ΚΑΛΛΙΚΟΜΟΙ ΚΟΥΡΑΙ ΔΙΟΣ ΩΡΧΗΣΑΝΤ ΕΛΑΦΡΩΣ

143. *Hunting dog.*
702. *Hermes and the Graces.*
675. *Kore (from Chios).*

The happy face of the Kore, with the archaic smile, the complicated, decorative hairdo of her forehead, the rich, heavy braids, which fall majestically on her shoulders and breast, the bright colors of her pleated dress, and the movement of her body under its rich jewelery and ornaments compose a piece of work full of freshness, youth and female coquetry.

643. *Head of Kore:* The head of a Kore of the end of the 6th century B.C. is unique in beauty and tenderness. The finesse of the outline, the velvet skin, the expressive eyes, the accentuated cheekbones, the face with its strange smile, at the same time both sad and joyful, create an unusually attractive personality.

682. *Kore:* An attic archaic statue of a Kore, of the end of the 6th century B.C. (520 B.C.), with an intense ionic influence. The Kore, with an effusive affected stylishness, an extremely tall and disproportionate body, and a face full of angles, does not create a friendly predisposition towards her. She is cold and aloof. The rich, multi-colored, ornate jewelry show her to be vain, but the repulsing expression of her face and eyes do not allow one to be attracted to her.

674. *Kore:* The statue of this Kore is the work of an outstanding artist of 500 B.C. The beautifully shaped, enigmatic face, with the intense slanting eyes, is harmoniously framed by the artistically worked mass of hair, which ends in ringlets, resting symmetrically on her breast. Preserving remnants of its strong colors, the dress of the Kore does not hug her body tightly, while the well-known traditional archaic smile is absent from her well-shaped enigmatic face, as though she were seeking another expression and a new understanding of the approaching trend in sculpture.

684. *Kore:* The statue of a Kore (approximately 490 B.C.) is, probably, a more recent piece of work of the artist, who created the Kore number 674. This Kore is characterized by a perfect suppleness of both body and face. She, as well as, the previous Kore, the works of the end of the Archaic period in art, keep many of the old characteristics, but open the way and foretell the outstanding characteristics of another newer trend, which is being born during the years of the Persian Wars, the "Severe Style".

670. *Kore:* She wears only an ionic chiton, which loosely covers her body. She is raising her skirt, in front, with her left hand. Two layers of deeply waved hair and a diadem encircles her head, while two sets of four tresses frame her neck. Traces of decoration around the neckline of the chiton and the central fold of the skirt are visible. About 500 B.C.

685. *Kore:* Lithe, and well-proportioned, this Kore has the attractive slenderness of a leaf-stalk in her bearing. It is an Attic piece of work with ionic influence of the decade of 500 - 490 B.C. The Kore had both arms bending at the elbows, extending in front of her, as contrasted with most other Korae, who hold the folds of their garment with their one hand.

76

684. *Kore.*
682. *Kore.*
643. *Head of Kore.*

684

682

643

670. *Kore.*
685. *Kore.*
674. *Kore.*

670   685

Room V

683. *Kore:* This Kore, which has survived in its entirety, is one of the most strange of the entire collection, with her disproportionate midget-like body, the heavy, strangely rendered expression of her face, her shapeless clothing, and the pointed, outdated red shoes. Furthermore, the Kore brings forward her right instead of her left leg, lifts her dress up with her right hand, while she holds a bird (a dove) with the left. This is a piece of work of the end of the 6th century B.C. (of approximately 510 B.C.).

631C. *Giant:* One of the Giants of the eastern pediment of the "archaios neos", the one which had been placed at the left corner. The pediment, a piece of work of 525 B.C., represented a scene from the Gigantomachy. The Giant, naked, with long hair and a round face, bending his left leg at the knee, and stretching his right leg behind him, rests on the tips of his toes, and carefully prepares to enter the fight which is taking place at the center of the pediment. The respective Giant, at the right corner, is also making the same preparations.

Zeus and Athena are standing at the center of the pediment, each facing the opposite side, fighting one of the Giants. Engelados is Athena's opponent. Next to the two pairs, to their right and left, one may see one more pair of entangled God and Giant. Only a few pieces have survived from this pedimental composition, the most significant being the statue of Athena, which was lately put together in its correct position by John Miliades.

681. *The Antenor Kore:* A large statue of a Kore with an inscription on its base, which mentions the name of the donor, the potter Nearchos, and of the artist-creator Antenor, a monumental piece of work of the archaic attic sculptural work of approximately 520 B.C.

The moulding of the body with the broad shoulders, the strong arms, and full breasts, lend the Kore intense nobility, which reaches its apex in the severe unaffected simplicity of the head. The head, with its strong, geometric outline, the diadem at the top, and the ringlets which frame it gracefully, emphasize its greatness and fill it with a divine beauty. The eyes of the Kore had been fashioned from embedded rock crystal and lit her face with their radiance. The folds of her dress have been worked with exceptional mastery, and are especially deep and sharp along the perpendicular axis of the statue.

Alcove

621. *Small male head:* A small male head of a statue, which was less than life-like in size, probably of a helmet-bearing rider, is a piece of work of approximately 500 B.C. A cutting glance and intelligence characterize the visage.

641. *Head of a small Kore:* The head of a small statue of a Kore, the work of cycladic art of approximately 490 B.C. The small face, with the innocent look and the pure smile, is diffused with girlish tenderness and charm.

6447. *Bronze wild boar:* A minuscule bronze wild boar, that is running on a narrow curved plinth, was an ornament of a large bronze vessel of the 5th century B.C.

681

681. *The Antenor Kore.*
— *Athena from the pediment of the Gigantomachy.*

Room VI

689. *The Blond youth:* An exceptional head of a youth of the era of the Persian Wars (485 - 480 B.C.), is known as the head of the "blond youth" because, when it was found, its hair had a deep-yellow color, of which traces may still be seen today. It is most probably an attic piece of work, rather than a Peloponnesian (Argive) one, and it is possible that it had been executed by the sculptor-teacher of Phidias.

A romantic wariness, and an adolescent melancholy, which reach the border of gravity, are characteristic of the youth who is in agony over life and the future.

695. *Contemplative Athena:* A relief of the period of the "Severe Style" (460 B.C.), Athena is resting on her overturned spear with her left arm, in a posture of contemplation, barefoot and simple in her doric peplos, looking rather like a mortal young lady. Her symbol, the Corinthian helmet, proves her divine identity. Many ideas have been brought forth and many explanations have been stated about what the goddess is thinking, and about the symbolic meaning attributed to the stele, which is in front of her, and she is contemplating over. However, that which is quite evident, and we can obviously see, is the artist's intention of carving his goddess with artistic sensitivity, and making the beloved divinity more accessible and human.

698. *The Kritios boy:* This youth, made of Parian marble, a product of Kritios' workshop who, along with Nisiotes, created the second group of tyrannicides, is a masterpiece of the beginning of the "Severe Style", having been completed just before 480 B.C., since it was found in the stratum of the Persian destruction. The statue, most probably, depicts an athlete and intends to render the perfection of a youthful male, as best it can. Therefore, the deep thoughtfulness and spirituality which dominate its contemporary "blond youth", are absent from this youth. A tender finesse is characteristic of the features of his face, while a wonderful, soft resilience is diffused throughout its entire body.

67. *Painted plaque:* A rare specimen of painting on a plaque, probably of architectural function. A naked warrior attacks towards the left. He is armed with helmet, spear and shield. The name Megakles, which was painted above, was erased and the name Glaukytes substituted. It is most probable that the plaque is depicting the Alcmeonid Megakles, who was ostracized and left Athens in 486. At this time his name must have been erased and replaced by the other one. It is possible that the plaque is the work of the vase-painter Euthymides (510 - 500 B.C.).

686 *and* **609.** *The Euthydikos Kore:* The statue of a Kore, an attic piece of work of approximately 490 B.C. Extant, today, we have the upper part of her body, from the waist up, and the legs, from below the middle of the thighs, with a plinth, which is stuck with lead, on the inscribed base of the statue. According to the inscription, the statue had been dedicated to the goddess by one Euthydikos, son of Thaliarchos.

The Kore, while keeping the traditional elements of the archaic technique, demonstrates the new concept of life and art, which is expressed during this period.

The traditional smile is absent from the chubby face of the Kore, while the full lips, in combination with her heavy look, make her look dejected. She is justifiably called "the

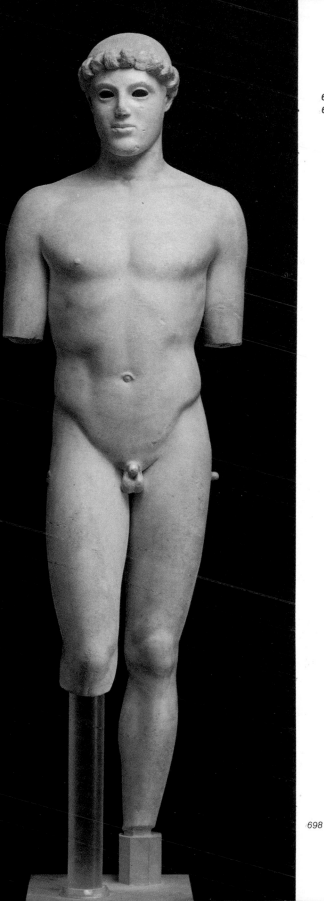

698. *The Kritios Boy.*
689. *The Blond Youth.*

698

689

angry one". The transparency of her dress, over the projecting left leg of the Kore, has been depicted with exceptional success.

697. *Front part of a horse:* A horse of exceptional artistic value, dedicated to Athena, a piece of work of the decade of 490 - 480 B.C. The front part is extant, and shows that it stood alone, without a rider, itself being an honorary symbol of its victory during a race of racing horses alone. The outlines, the surfaces, and the anatomical details of the horse have been depicted with unsurpassable finesse and unique sensitivity. The raised ears, the open nostrils, the half-open mouth, the hoof of its lifted right leg, which paws the earth ready to dash forward demonstrate a liveliness, a high-strung nervous-ness, and a spirited restlessness; all signs of strength and dignity over the victory, which has already been won, and over the next one which is forthcoming.

Room VII

855. *Head of Iris:* The head of Iris in high relief, from slab V of the eastern frieze of the Parthenon, which is located in the British Museum. The face of the goddess is dignified and radiant with a pure, virgin beauty. Holding up her hair, with her left hand, she is preparing to receive the procession.

705. *A scene from the Centauromachy:* A practically intact metope from the southern flank of the Parthenon. A Centaur is grabbing a Lapith woman from the waist, while she is resisting and pushing him away with all her strength, as he, in a violent effort, is attempting to carry her on his back. The subject of this representation gives movement and rhythm to this relief, while the folds of the clothing and the nakedness of the body are especially accentuated.

Room VIII

864. *The Hydriaphoroi:* A slab from the frieze of the northern flank of the Parthenon. Three "hydriaphoroi" (water bearers), with the tunics falling full of folds, walk on steadily and calmly carrying water-jugs on their shoulders, while a fourth one is bending, in preparation of lifting his own. The scene is an instantaneous event, among the total scene of the Panathenaic procession.

857. *Youths driving cattle:* A slab of the frieze of the northern flank, one of the most beautiful of the Parthenon. Three youths are driving two bulls to sacrifice. The first two youths, wearing long tunics, follow — with lowered heads, and in a manner befitting a sacred moment — the unsuspecting bull, while a third one, behind them, with the tunic off the shoulder, is attempting to pacify the enraged second bull, which is resisting, as though it was aware of its fate.

960. *Youths leading rams:* The largest part of a slab from the frieze of the northern flank of the Parthenon. Three youths (colonials-metics?) are leading rams to sacrifi-ce. They are wearing tunics, and two of them are looking at each other, carrying on a

695. Contemplative Athena. 6

697

686

discussion, while, in contrast, a third one is looking behind. An instantaneous event of the simple, and real, everyday pastoral life.

856. *East frieze of the Parthenon. Gods:* Slab of the east frieze of the Parthenon with Poseidon, Apollo, Artemis and Aphrodite seating on stools.

At the left Poseidon looks toward the procession of Panathenaia and wears a himation, which leaves the upper body free. The painted trident is entirely worn away.

Apollo is turning his head to speak to Poseidon. His himation falls in soft folds. The holes in his hair testify that a wreath of gilded bronze leaves was fastened on his head.

Beside Apollo there is Artemis, peacefully seated. Her hair is bounded up in a sakkos, her chiton reveals her shoulder and she holds on to Aphrodite with her right hand.

Only small fragments from Aphrodite are visible: parts of her head, her chiton and himation and part of her stool.

This particular part of the frieze, with the inspired differentiation of pose, drapery and character of the figures and the perfection of every detail, is probably the work of the sculptor Alcamenes, Phidias' greatest follower.

863. *Riders:* A slab from the northern flank of the Parthenon, which is practically intact. The scene depicted is majestic, with a rhythmic musicality, and is one of the most beautiful of the entire frieze. The bodies of the youths and horses, the human heads, and the heads of the animals, the arms of the young men, and the legs of the horses, entangled with pleated tunics, the manes and the flying tails, compose a masterpiece, unique in conception, mastery, inspiration and movement. The youth who is walking among the riders, and is looking behind towards the advancing procession, is the master of ceremonies, and regulates the order of the procession with a wave of his hand.

862. *Riders:* A slab from the frieze of the northern flank of the Parthenon. Four riders, who are galloping forcefully, are represented here. The force of the gallop is declared with intensity, by the nervousness of the movement, the legs of the horses who look as though they are not stepping on the earth, while, in contrast, the riders, sitting calmly and preoccupied on their horses, are being led to the fulfillment of their sacred duty.

973. *The "Sandalbinder Nike":* A slab with a representation of Nike, from the parapet of the temple of Athena Nike, probably from the southern flank. In order to step on the altar barefoot, with her left foot, Nike bends her body over to take off the sandal of her uplifted right foot, with her right hand. This masterpiece in relief is one of the characteristic examples of the "Rich Style". The artist was one of the best of his time, and rendered the female body, which is outlined, practically naked, beneath the transparent pleated dress, with unsurpassed dexterity, unusual finesse and sensitivity, the climax of the relationship between the body and the clothing which covers it. This relief is one of the rarest and unrepeatable creations of ancient sculpture.

Room IX

1331. *Alexander:* The head of Alexander the Great at an early age, most probably the

864. *The Hydriaphoroi.*
857. *Youths driving cattle.*

work of the sculptor Leochares, who executed it after 338 B.C., immediately after Alexander's arrival in Athens, after the battle of Chaironeia.

1313. *Philosopher's head:* It is a head from a portrait bust. The portrait, with the wide open eyes, the rather bitter sense of life, the flowing locks that frame the face, bears witness to the vitality and strength of Athenian tradition even toward the end of the ancient world.

It is the work of the first half of the 5th century A.D. and probably represents the neoplatonic philosopher Plutarch, who died in 431 - 432 A.D.

1339. *The Lenormant relief:* Fragment of a relief representing an Athenian trireme. In the oarports nine oarsmen lean forward and row hard. On the right above a youthful figure, the hero Paralos, the inventor of travel by boat is probably depicted..

The trireme would be the Paralos, the sacred trireme of the Athenian state, which travelled for important missions. About the end of the 5th century B.C.

960. Youths leading rams.
856. East frieze of the Parthenon.Gods.

960

856

1331

862. *Riders.*

1331. *Head of Alexander.*

1313. *Philosopher's head.*
— *Athena from the pediment of the Gigantomachy.*

BIBLIOGRAPHY

GENERAL WORKS

O. Jahn and A. Michaelis, *Arx Athenarum a Pausania descripta* [3], Bonnae 1901.
P. Kavvadias and G. Kawerau, *Die Ausgrabung der Akropolis*, Athen 1906.
W. Kolbe, Die Neugestaltung der Akropolis nach den Perserkriegen, *Jahrbuch d. Deutschen Instituts* 1936, p. 1 ff.
E. Langlotz and W.H. Schuchhardt, *Archaische Plastik auf der Akropolis* [2], Frankfurt a. M. 1943.
Sp. Iakovidis, Ἡ μυκηναϊκή ἀκρόπολις τῶν Ἀθηνῶν, Ἀθῆναι 1962.
John Miliades, *A Short Guide to the Museum of the Acropolis*, Athens 1965.
John Travlos, *Pictorial Dictionary of Anc. Athens*, London 1971.
The pyblication of *"Pausanias Periegesis" (description)*, the "Attica" (Athens, 1974, Ekdotike Athenon S.A.), with a detailed, and complete annotation of the ancient text, by Nicholaos Papahatzis.
Maria Brouskaris, *Descriptive Catalogue of the Museum of the Acropolis, Athens 1974*.

SELECTED WORKS

PARTHENON, HEKATOMPEDON AND THE ANCIENT TEMPLE OF ATHENA

W.B. Dinsmoor, The Date of the Older Parthenon, *Amer. Journ. of Arch.* 1934, 408 ff. 1935, 508 f.
— The Hekatompedon on the Athenian Acropolis, *Amer. Journ. of Arch.* 1947, 109 ff.
W. Dörpfeld, Parthenon I, II und III, *Amer. Journ. of Arch.* 1935, 497 ff.
— Der alte Athenatempel auf der Akropolis, *Ath. Mitt.* 1897, 159 ff.
W.B. Dinsmoor, The Burning of the Opisthodomos at Athens, *Amer. Journ. of Arch.* 1932, 143f. and 307f.
A. K. Orlandos, Ἡ ἀρχιτεκτονική τοῦ Παρθενῶνος, Α΄ Πίνακες, Ἀθῆναι 1976.

ERECHTHEION

L.D. Caskey, H.N. Fowler, *The Erechtheum*, 1927
W. Dörpfeld and H. Schleif, *Erechtheion*, Berlin 1942
N. Kontoleon, Τὸ Ἐρέχθειον ὡς οἰκοδόμημα χθονίας λατρείας, Ἀθῆναι 1949.

PROPYLAEA

G.Ph. Stevens, The Periclean Entrance Court of the Acropolis of Athens, *Hesperia* 1936, 446 f. 1946, 73 f.
W. Dörpfeld, Die Propyläen der Akropolis von Athen, *Ath. Mitt.* 1885, 38 f.
C.H. Weller, The Pre - periclean Propylon of the Acropolis of Athens, *Amer. Journ. of Arch.* 1904, 35 f.

TEMPLE OF ATHENA NIKE

A.K. Orlandos, Zum Tempel der Athena Nike, *Ath. Mitt.* 1915, 27 f.
N. Balanos, Ἡ νέα ἀναστήλωσις τοῦ ναοῦ τῆς Ἀθηνᾶς Νίκης, Ἀρχ. Ἐφ. 1937, 776 f.
G. Welter, Vom Nikepyrgos, *Ath. Mitt.* 1923, 190ff, *Arch. Anz.* 1939, 1 ff.

BRAURONION - CHALKOTHECA

F. Versakis, *Das Brauronion und die Chalkotek im Zeitalter der Antoninen*, Athen 1910.

ASKLEPIEION - THEATER OF DIONYSOS - ODEION OF HERODES ATTICOS AND ODEION OF PERIKLES

F. Versakis, Μνημεῖα τῶν νοτίων προπόδων τῆς Ἀκροπόλεως, Ἀρχ. Ἐφ. 1912, 161 ff.
P. Girard, *L' Asclépieion d' Athènes*, Paris 1881.
I. Travlos, Τὸ Ἀσκληπιεῖον τῶν Ἀθηνῶν, Ἀρχ. Ἐφ. 1939 - 1941, 60 f.
A.W. Pickard - Cambridge, *The Theatre of Dionysus in Athens*, Oxford 1946.
J.T. Allen, On the Odeum and the Periclean Reconstruction of the Theater, *Univ. Cal. Publ. Class. Arch.* 1941, 173 ff.
W.P. Tuckermann, *Das Odeum des Herodes Atticus und der Regilla in Athen*, Bonn 1868.

CHORAGIC MONUMENTS

W.B. Dinsmoor, The Choragic Monument of Nicias, *Amer. Journ. of Arch.* 1910, 459 ff.
G. Welter, Das choragische Denkmal des Thrasyllos, *Arch. Anz.* 1938, 33 ff.

ACROPOLIS OF ATHENS AND ITS MONUMENTS

1. Monument of Lysicrates
2. Odeion of Pericles
3 - 6. Sanctuary of Dionysos Eleuthereus
    3. Old temple of Dionysos Eleuthereus
    4. New temple of Dionysos Eleuthereus
    5. Altar of Dionysos Eleuthereus
    6. Stoa of the sanctuary of Dionysos Eleuthereus
7. Scene of the theater of Dionysos Eleuthereus
8. Orchestra of the theater of Dionysos Eleuthereus
9. Choragic monument of Thrasyllos
10. Choragic columns above the monument of Thrasyllos
11. Choragic monument of Nikias
12 - 17. Shrine of Asklepios
    12. Temple of Asklepios
    13. Altar of the shrine
    14. Stoa
    15. Square room of the shrine
    16. Southern stoa of the shrine
    17. Ionic stoa of the shrine
18. Fountain (of Alkippe?)
19. Temple of Themis
20. "Hippolyteion" (shrine dedicated to Hippolytos)
21. Stoa of Eumenes
22. Odeion of Herodes Atticos
23. Sanctuary of the "Nymphe"
24. Roman buildings
25. Shrines on the southwestern end of the Acropolis
26. Clepsydra
27. Shrine of Apollo
28. Shrine of Zeus Olympios
29. Shrine of Pan
30. Shrine of Aphrodite and Eros
31. "Aglaureion"
32. "Anakeion"
33. Beulé Gate
34. Altar of Apollo Agyieus
35. Shrine of Athena Pylatis
36. Pedestal of Eumenes - quadriga of Agrippas
37. Propylaea of Mnesicles
38. Pinacotheca
39. Building with two chambers
40. Temple of Athena Nike
41. Shrine of Brauronia Artemis
42. Chalcotheca
43. Parthenon
44. Temple of Roma and Augustus
45. Shrine of Pandion
46. Shrine of Zeus Polieus
47. Shrine of "Gaia (earth) Karpophoros (fruitful)"
48. Altar of Athena
49. Ancient temple of Athena
50. Erechtheion
51. Pandroseion
52. Arrephorion
53. Athena Promachos